CAPITAL AND CREDIT IN BRITISH OVERSEAS TRADE

Capital and Credit in British Overseas Trade: The View from the Chesapeake, 1700–1776

Jacob M. Price

HARVARD UNIVERSITY PRESS

Cambridge, Massachusetts, and London, England   1980

Library of Congress Cataloging in Publication Data

Price, Jacob M
    Capital and credit in British overseas trade.

    Bibliography: p.
    Includes index.
        1. Capital—Chesapeake Bay region—History.   2. Credit—Chesapeake
Bay region—History.   3. Capital—Great Britain—History.   4. Credit—
Great Britain—History.   5. Chesapeake Bay region—Commerce—
History.   6. Great Britain—Colonies—America—Commerce—History.   I.
Title.
HC110.C3P75   332'.041'0975518   80-13815
ISBN 0-674-09480-8

To the memory of my mother
ALICE PIKE PRICE
(1898–1972)

Acknowledgments

I WOULD LIKE to thank the librarians and archivists of all the repositories mentioned in the notes. I am particularly indebted to the staffs of the Public Record Office, the Scottish Record Office, the National Library of Scotland, the Strathclyde Regional Archives, the Bristol Archives Office, and the Maryland Hall of Records. For permission to consult their family muniments and business archives, I am highly indebted to Sir James Hunter Blair, bart., Major Richard Oswald, the Bank of England, the Bank of Scotland, the Royal Bank of Scotland, Barclays Bank Ltd., the National Westminster Bank Ltd., Messrs. Coutts & Company, and the former Glyn, Mills & Company, Ltd. Quotation from *The Papers of Thomas Jefferson*, volume 10 (1954), edited by Julian P. Boyd, is by permission of Princeton University Press. Transcripts of Crown-copyright records in the Public Record Office appear by permission of the Controller of H. M. Stationery Office. I also wish to thank the directors of the William L. Clements Library, Ann Arbor, and the Maryland Historical Society, Baltimore, for permission to make extended quotations from records in their custody.

This project was aided by grants from the American Council of Learned Societies, the National Endowment for the Humanities, and the Horace H. Rackham School of Graduate Studies of the University of Michigan. This version of the study was written at the Rockefeller Foundation's Villa Serbelloni, Bellagio, Italy, in 1978 and owes much to the invitation of the foundation and to the hospitality of the staff at the villa.

An earlier and much shorter version of this study was given as a lecture at Bowling Green State University in 1970. It was published by the university in a volume entitled *Of Mother Country and Plantations: Proceedings of the Twenty-Seventh Conference in Early American History*, edited by Virginia Bever Platt and David Curtis Skaggs (Bowling Green, Ohio, 1971).

I am indebted to Professors Stanley Engerman and John Shy, who read the draft manuscript and made valuable suggestions, and to Professor Leslie S. Pressnell for helpful comments on Chapter 5.

Contents

TABLES

CAPITAL AND CREDIT IN BRITISH OVERSEAS TRADE

ABBREVIATIONS

AO	Archives Office
BL	British Library, London
LC	Library of Congress (Manuscripts Division), Washington, D.C.
MdHR	Maryland Hall of Records, Annapolis
MdHS	Maryland Historical Society, Baltimore
NLS	National Library of Scotland, Edinburgh
P.C.C.	Prerogative Court of Canterbury
PRO	Public Record Office, London
RO	Record Office
SRA	Strathclyde Regional Archives, Glasgow
SRO	Scottish Record Office, Edinburgh
VaHS	Virginia Historical Society, Richmond
VaSL	Virginia State Library, Richmond

1

Introduction

RECENT SCHOLARSHIP has devoted considerable attention to the problem of capital and credit in the early stages of the Industrial Revolution. Such work has tended to emphasize the relatively small capital needs and resources of the earliest factory owners and the relatively greater importance of working capital than of fixed capital. Capital expansion took place largely through the reinvestment of profits. With his own rather meager capital very often substantially tied up in his modest plant and equipment, the early industrialist depended for much of his vital working capital on loans (very often from within the family) and on commercial credit from merchants and others with whom he dealt. In this literature, the merchant appears fleetingly as something of a deus ex machina who solves problems of capital shortage by supplying the early industrialist with raw materials on credit and timely payments for his manufactures. Little attention is given in most of the literature to the way in which the merchant obtained the resources with which he helped the early industrialist. Merchants are simply taken to be wealthier than operators of early cotton spinning mills.[1]

There were of course some very wealthy merchants in the eighteenth century, particularly those who were involved in the founding of the three great moneyed companies—the Bank of England, the new East India Company, the South Sea Company—and other such ventures. However, merchants generally and foreign traders specifically were not strikingly wealthy.[2] Those who were very well off tended to buy land and gradually shift from trade to a gentler status. It is therefore well worth asking what kind of capital resources merchants in foreign trade commanded in the eighteenth century. How much wealth of their own did they bring to trade? To what extent were they able to build up their capital by reinvesting their profits in their businesses? How much extra working capital were they able to obtain on loan? From whom and on what terms? To what extent were they, too, dependent on commercial credit? On what terms and from whom?

British commerce in the eighteenth century embraced most of the maritime world from the Gulf of Finland to the Gulf of Honduras and from Hudson's Bay to the South China Sea. In this monograph I shall be concerned only with those trades open to the ordinary merchant and not with those dominated by monopoly joint-stock societies such as the East India and Hudson's Bay companies. Within nonmonopolized commerce, I shall concentrate upon the American trades, particularly that to the Chesapeake tobacco colonies of Viriginia and Maryland. There are several reasons for this beyond the obvious limitations of time and space. The American trades were relatively capital-intensive; they also involved very extensive advances of credit. At the beginning of the American Revolution, credits of several million pounds were still outstanding. After the return of peace in 1783, these prewar debts were the subject of treaty clauses in 1783, 1794, and 1802, the results of extensive diplomatic and administrative attention. These efforts have left behind a much more extensive documentation on the capital and credit structure of the North America trades than that available for any other contemporary trade. Within the North America trade, that to the Chesapeake appears to have been disproportionately capital-intensive and credit-prone. Its debt problems consequently left an even more substantial body of postwar documentation than did those of the trades to the other former colonies. The Chesapeake trade admittedly had at least one atypical institutional development, the rather precocious Glasgow store system, which produced some unusually large firms on the eve of the Revolution. Even the three largest of these, however, were probably not exceptionally large by the standards of the greatest West India firms of the time. The Chesapeake firms shared with other North America and West India firms the common problems of utilizing internal British credit institutions to support extensive credit commitments abroad. These same credit arrangements appear to have been typical of some if perhaps not all European trades, as well as of most of the domestic trade.

While concentrating upon the trades to Virginia and Maryland, I have, wherever possible, used material from other trades in order to put the Chesapeake trade in context and suggest its typical or atypical features. This study would have been infinitely easier had there been equivalent studies of capital and credit problems in other branches of British external (or even internal) trade. Until such investigations are made, generalizations from the Chesapeake to other trades can only rest on a provisional and somewhat impressionistic basis.

Though I investigate here in some detail the capital and credit problems of the Chesapeake-British trade, I have not attempted a general institutional or serial history of that trade. That will have to await a later study.

2

The Problem of Debt Viewed from the Chesapeake

DEBT AND DEBTORS are hardly neglected themes in American history, least of all in that of the period preceding the American Revolution. The importance of these topics for prerevolutionary Virginia in particular has often been recognized, though rarely analyzed systematically. A common view of the problem derives perhaps from a well-known passage by Jefferson written in 1786:

> Virginia certainly owed two millions sterling to Great Britain at the conclusion of the war. Some have conjectured the debt as high as three millions. I think that state owed near as much as all the rest put together. This is to be ascribed to peculiarities in the tobacco trade. The advantages made by the British merchants on the tobaccoes consigned to them were so enormous that they spared no means of increasing those consignments. A powerful engine for this purpose was the giving good prices and credit to the planter, till they got him more immersed in debt than he could pay without selling his lands or slaves. They then reduced the prices given for his tobacco so that let his shipments be ever so great, and his

demand of necessaries ever so oeconomical, they never permitted him to clear off his debt. These debts had become hereditary from father to son for many generations, so that the planters were a species of property annexed to certain mercantile houses in London.[1]

Quite apart from Jefferson's paranoia about snares and enticements and manipulated prices, he presented the problem entirely from the standpoint of a consigning planter like himself or his father. In fact, in the decades preceding the Revolution, less than two-fifths (perhaps only a quarter) of the tobacco arriving in Britain came on consignment from planters and native merchants combined. The other three-fifths or more was bought in Virginia and Maryland and shipped on the account of merchants in Britain.[2] Nevertheless, as "sellers in the country" could be as debt-encumbered as consignors to Britain, there was a substantial element of truth in Jefferson's depiction of the intensity of the debt problem in Virginia.

In 1790–91, a committee of London and Glasgow merchants prepared an inventory of all the prewar mercantile debts still owed by "Citizens of the United States of America to the Merchants and Traders of Great Britain" (table 1). Out of a total claimed of £4,984,655, no less than £2.3 million or 46.25 percent was owed by residents of Virginia, while Maryland accounted for £571,455 (11.46 percent) and North Carolina for £379,344 (7.6 percent). Together, the three tobacco colonies were responsible for 65.3 percent of all sums claimed. As this account was made up as of January 1, 1790, it included about fourteen years' interest (at 5 percent), which must be deducted from the absolute figures to get the pre-1776 debt upon which the claims were based. If it is assumed

Table 1. Pre-1776 colonial debt (sterling) still owed to British creditors in 1790, with interest.

Location of creditors	Total	Virginia	Maryland	North Carolina	South Carolina and Georgia	Middle colonies	New England
London	£2,324,653	£390,225	£310,408	£34,701	£844,072	£364,344	£380,903
Bristol	104,583	80,134	16,227	0	8,222	0	0
Liverpool	127,566	125,934	197	0	0	1,435	0
Whitehaven and Workington	30,309	28,638	715	662	0	224	70
Glasgow and Greenock	2,212,943	1,605,507	242,052	343,309	11,954	8,202	1,919
Kilmarnock	20,810	20,810	0	0	0	0	0
Leeds	92,759	54,161	1,856	672	456	30,866	4,748
Chester	71,032	0	0	0	71,032	0	0
Total	4,984,655	2,305,409	571,455	379,344	935,736	405,071	387,640

Source: PRO, P.R.O. 30/8/343, fols. 167–9. I am indebted to Mrs. Katherine Kellock of Washington, D.C., for this reference. See also P.R.O. 30/8/344, fol. 45.

that the interest was compounded annually, 49.5 percent should be deducted; but if it is assumed that the interest was not compounded in preparing the account, only 41.2 percent need be deducted to obtain the prewar equivalent. There is in fact considerable evidence that merchants in the 1780s did *not* use compound interest in preparing debt claims. The deduction of simple interest reduces the total prewar debt still outstanding in 1790 to £2,932,150 (table 2) and the three tobacco colonies' 65.3 percent to £1,915,417.[3] These figures do not, however, represent the total prewar debt owed at the peak (about 1774). Some merchants and planters voluntarily settled with their British creditors in the 1780s, particularly those desirous of reestablishing credit in Great Britain. (Outside Virginia, others were obliged to settle when state courts—for example, those of Maryland in 1787— recognized the validity of prewar bonds and other specialties securing debts to British merchants.)[4] More important, during the last year before the war (the twelve or so months ending September 1775), importations into the colonies from Britain were prohibited by Congress, though exports to Britain were permitted. At that time, we learn from a later writer, "the factors, whom the Glasgow merchants had established in America, by their prudent exertions, and the friendly terms on which they generally were with the planters [perhaps not all of them], had been enabled to make large remittances to their constituents, before matters were brought to the last extremity."[5] According to the well-informed Bristol merchant Richard Champion, the amounts owing from America were reduced from £6 million in December 1774 to £2 million in December 1775.[6] This estimate of repayment

Table 2. Pre-1776 colonial debt (sterling) still owed to British creditors in 1790, interest deducted.

Location of creditors	Total	Virginia	Maryland	North Carolina	South Carolina and Georgia	Middle colonies	New England
London	£1,367,443	£229,544	£182,593	£20,412	£496,513	£214,320	£224,061
Bristol	61,519	47,138	9,545	0	4,836	0	0
Liverpool	75,039	76,079	116	0	0	844	0
Whitehaven and Workington	17,829	16,846	421	389	0	132	41
Glasgow and Greenock	1,301,731	944,416	142,383	201,947	7,032	4,825	1,128
Kilmarnock	12,241	12,241	0	0	0	0	0
Leeds	54,564	31,859	1,092	396	268	18,156	2,793
Chester	41,784	0	0	0	41,784	0	0
Total	2,932,150	1,356,123	336,150	223,144	550,433	238,277	228,023

Source: Adapted from table 1, assuming 14 years' simple interest at 5% p.a.

may be excessive, for the 1790 claims showed almost £3 million (principal) still owing from before the war. Against this last figure, however, must be set the understandable tendency of creditors, when dealing with the government after the war, to represent all their prewar debts as "good," though many of these even in 1775 must have been classifiable as "doubtful" or "desperate." All that can be said with any assurance is that something near or over £2 million sterling was owed to British merchants by the three tobacco colonies on the eve of the war, and that Virginia and Maryland alone owed at least £1,692,000. Virginia, with about 21 percent of the population of the thirteen colonies, accounted for something like 46 percent of the total colonial debt, while Virginia and Maryland combined, with 30 percent of the population and 29.5 percent of imports from Britain (1770–1774), accounted for about 57.4 percent of the debt.[7]

The pattern of debt was of long standing in British-American trade,[8] though the share of the Chesapeake seems to have been growing. Estimates of the total debt owing from Virginia and Maryland rose from £50,000 in 1664 to £1 million in 1757.[9] At the time of the Stamp Act hearings in 1766, the "Committee of Merchants of London Trading to North America" suggested that debts from North America owed to British merchants came to something approaching £5 million sterling:

To London	£2,900,000
To Bristol	800,000
To Glasgow (Virginia and Maryland only)	500,000
To Liverpool	150,000
To Manchester	100,000
Total	4,450,000

And to this must be added the "Sums due to Lancaster, Whitehaven, Birmingham, Sheffield, Leeds, Norwich, Wakefield, Halifax [etc.]."

The Glasgow estimate of £500,000, restricted to Virginia and Maryland, came from the cautious John Glassford.[10] About the same time, John Brown, another Glasgow merchant, put the total owing to the Clyde from all North America at near £1 million.[11] Brown's more global figure is not only more useful but also more consistent with other scraps of evidence. If we assume that his sum of near £1 million meant at least £900,000 and substitute that figure for Glassford's and, at the same time, allow £250,000 for all the lesser English and Scottish centers for which figures are missing, we get a total debt of £5.1 million for 1766, roughly consistent with Champion's estimate of £6 million in 1774. In between, the only big change came in Glasgow, which in 1766 had perhaps £900,000 owing from all North America, but which (according to the 1790 claim) had in 1776—even after all the 1774–1775 repayments—£1.3 million owing from the former thirteen colonies, of which £1,087,000 was accounted for by Virginia and Maryland. Such a growth in debt, though atypical, was not inconsistent with the 53 percent increase in Scottish exports to the thirteen colonies between the periods 1761–1765 and 1770–1774 or the 49.4 percent increase in Scottish tobacco imports during the same years.[12]

Not only Glassford's, but all these figures present problems. They must be used cautiously not only because many of them are only estimates, but also because they are of different dates and describe constantly changing economies. Since debt was a derivative of Anglo-American trade, its increase might only mean that British-American trade was increasing. The degree to which this was so is examined in table 3. The relative burden of the debt to Britain seems to have shown a significant upward drift, reaching an apparent peak for the thirteen colonies in 1766, when it was 2.52 times the value of annual imports from Britain. This was alleviated somewhat in subsequent years, helped in varying degrees by the nonimportation bans of 1769–70 and 1774 and by higher prices for tobacco in the late 1760s and for wheat in both the late 1760s and early 1770s. The apparently substantial reduction of debt by the thirteen colonies between 1774 and 1776 did not extend pari passu to Virginia and Maryland, where tobacco prices were declining between 1770 and 1774, so that the Chesapeake colonies in 1776 still owed Britain the equivalent of almost twice their annual average imports.[13]

The burden of this same debt would of course vary also with the size of the population that had to support it. This dimension of the problem is explored in table 4. The debt per head of the thirteen colonies peaked about 1766, with a very substantial reduction occurring between 1774 and 1776. This reduction was felt only weakly, if at all, in Virginia and Maryland, which in 1776 still had a debt per capita almost twice that of all thirteen colonies. If we deduct the Virginia and Maryland totals from those of all the colonies in 1776, we get an even more striking contrast. While these tobacco colonies owed an average of about £2.7.0 per head, the remaining eleven colonies had a British debt of £1,308,000 sterling or only about £0.14.4 per head. Although the debt problem in the Chesapeake may not have been significantly different

Table 3. Ratio of colonial debt to annual English or British exports to colonies (in thousands of pounds sterling).[a]

Year	Virginia and Maryland			Thirteen colonies		
	Colonial debt	Exports to colonies	Ratio	Colonial debt	Exports to colonies	Ratio
1664	£50	£76.5[b]	0.65	—	—	—
1757	1,000	529	1.89	—	—	—
1766	—	—	—	£5,000	£1,982	2.52
1774	—	—	—	6,000	2,843	2.11
1776	1,692+	903[c]	1.87+	3,000	3,061[c]	0.98

a. The debt figures are explained in the text; the export figures are from *Historical Statistics of the U.S.* (1976), II, 1176–78, 1189–91. They are for England alone in 1664, and for Great Britain from 1757 to 1776.

b. The value of exports to Virginia and Maryland in 1664 is an average of two calculations, assuming constant ratios. If we assume that English exports to Virginia and Maryland in 1663 and 1669 bore the same ratio to similar exports in 1699–1701 as English exports to all plantations at the later dates bore to the same exports at the earlier dates, we obtain the figure £75,000 for English exports to the two tobacco colonies in the 1660s. If, instead, we assume that English exports to Virginia and Maryland in 1663 and 1669 bore the same ratio to similar exports in 1699–1701 as English tobacco imports in the former years bore to tobacco imports in the latter, we obtain the figure £78,000 for English exports to the tobacco colonies in the 1660s. The mean of the two estimates is the £76,500 figure used for 1664. See Ralph Davis, "English Foreign Trade, 1660–1700," *Economic History Review*, 2d ser., 7 (1954), 150–166.

c. Average exports, 1770–1774.

Table 4. Relationship of colonial debt to colonial population.[a]

	Virginia and Maryland			Thirteen colonies		
Year	Debt (sterling)	Population	Debt per head	Debt (sterling)	Population	Debt per head
1664	£50,000	40,200	£1.25	—	—	—
1757	1,000,000	459,200	2.18	—	—	—
1766	—	—	—	£5,000,000	1,903,600	£2.63
1774	—	—	—	6,000,000	2,382,200	2.52
1776	1,692,000+	725,900	2.33+	3,000,000	2,507,900	1.20

a. The debt figures are explained in the text. The population figures are estimates obtained by interpolation from annual growth rates between the decennial figures given in *Historical Statistics of the United States* (1976), II, 1168.

from that in the other colonies in the 1750s and 1760s, it had become so by 1776. If we assume that the average Chesapeake household in 1776 consisted of 8.6 persons (family, servants, and slaves), then the debt to Britain per household at independence was about £20, less than the value of a single adult slave but still a significant burden.[14]

When one uses monetary data derived from widely separated periods of time, one may wonder whether monetary units continued to have the same value or whether their real value was significantly altered by price changes. This problem, however, can be ignored here because the prices of most of the goods exported from Britain to America between 1660 and 1790 fluctuated within fairly narrow limits without pronounced secular trends.[15] Only in the relatively rare instances where sums are cited before 1640 or after 1790 ought something to be allowed for the lower price levels of the earlier seventeenth century and the inflationary levels of the 1790s. (The more radical fluctuations in cereal prices are not too relevant here.)

Despite the crudeness of the data, the picture thus far is relatively clear. The debt of which Jefferson complained was not a figment of his imagination but a continuing feature of British-American trade, expanding as that trade expanded. Although it appears to have been a relatively light burden in most of the colonies, its weight was significantly heavier in the tobacco colonies, and noticeably so after the partial repayments of 1774–1776. How can we account for the disproportionate share of the tobacco colonies' indebtedness in the general pattern of colonial debt and for its illiquidity in the crisis of 1774–1776? Jefferson would have explained both as results of a conspiracy by British moneybags to ensnare the guileless planter into the cruel trap of easy credit. In truth, most contemporary correspondence reveals that merchants fully understood the uses of credit in creating a business clientele, but at the same time they were very unhappy about debts that took too long to collect and cautioned their agents about excessive advances. It is, however, of limited analytical utility to examine credit as only a moral relationship between the guileful and the guileless. Credit could also be a highly rational, mutually advantageous relationship for both clearsighted lenders and intelligent borrowers.

The nature of the colonial economy could make credit quite advantageous for the borrower under many sets of circumstances. If capital and labor were relatively scarce in the colonies, land was plentiful and cheap but was constantly increasing in value. Colonial planters and businessmen knew this and tried to buy cheap land whenever they could and to hold it for higher values later. It was rational to pay interest on debt rather than sell land if the interest paid (5 percent maximum in Britain) was less than the expected long-range annual increment in the value of land. Land, of course, increased most rapidly in value when "improved." Such improvement required scarce labor, either that of a tenant or that of the owner's own family, servants, or slaves. Servants or slaves usually were purchased for cash or on relatively short credit. However, the availability of "store credit" to provide for the normal needs of a household and plantation might enable a planter to divert cash toward the acquisition of servants or slaves. Even a tenant (as explained in chapter 7) could use and often needed store credit for the stake that would enable him to take up and improve a property and to survive until his crops, particularly his first crops, were in. For the planter big or small, there were of course dangers in credit, particularly when the assumption of credit involved informed judgment and might rest upon overly optimistic assumptions about the value of improvements and the future movement of prices.

For the merchant too, whether in the colonies or in Britain, credit was a rational but possibly dangerous practice. Credit greatly facilitated sales in all the colonies;[16] but overly generous credit could prove unrealizable, and seemingly mighty houses could fail with thousands of pounds in uncollectable debts among their "assets." Even so, British merchants may have been more prepared to extend long credits in the plantation colonies than in the northern or middle colonies because of the relatively greater ease of making remittances. Unlike their northern neighbors, the tobacco colonies and South Carolina produced commodities regularly wanted in northern Europe in quantity. (The transatlantic market for the fish and cereals of the more northerly colonies lay in southern Europe, and colonial wheat and flour were only admitted to Britain on a few occasions of bad harvest as in the late 1760s and early 1770s.) Thus credit to the residents of the Chesapeake and more southerly colonies, whether merchants or planters, seemed sound because these colonists had regular yearly incomes in the form of commodities (tobacco, rice, tar, and indigo in particular) that British factors (storekeepers) and colonial merchants could use as homeward remittances. Credit grew in the decades before the Revolution because the trades on which it was based grew (the tobacco trade tripling between the periods 1721–1725 and 1771–1775) and because the related growths of population, land values, and income made the planters much better credit risks than they had been formerly. One would naturally be prepared to advance much more to a man worth £10,000 than to one worth only £1,000. That growing wealth was the underlying cause of growing debt was recognized by none other than Jefferson's father-in-law, John Wayles, merchant and planter, who in 1766 wrote to his Bristol correspondents, Farell & Jones:

> It may be asked how come it that [British] Merch[an]ts are now more Embarrass'd [by debts owed them] than heretofore? The Cause is Obvious. The Planter having little or no Credit [in times past], the Merch[an]t was nothing in Advance, so no perplexity could Arise. Within these 25 Years, £1000 due to a Merch[an]t was looked upon as a sum immense and never to be got over. Ten times that sum is now spoke of with Indifference & thought no great burthen on some Estates. Indeed in that series of Time Property is become more Valuable & many Estates have increased more than tenfold. But then Luxury & expensive living have gone hand in hand with the increase of Wealth. In 1740 I don't remember to have seen such a thing as a turkey Carpet in the Country except a small thing in a bed chamber, Now nothing are so common as Turkey or Wilton Carpetts, the whole Furniture of the Roomes Elegant & every Appearance of Opulence. All this is in great Measure owing to the Cred[i]t which the Plant[e]rs have had from England & which has enabled them to Improve their Estates to the pitch they are Arrivd at, tho many are ignorant of the true Cause. In 1740, no man on this River made 100 hogsheads of tobacco: now not less than six exceed that Number.[17]

Wayles may have exaggerated the degree to which the trade of 1740 was debt-free, but he very clearly linked the growth of debt to the growth of income and wealth, which in turn was made possible by that very credit. Some scholars have suggested that this growth in wealth, income, and debt was greatly stimulated by the heavy issues of paper money during the Seven Years' War.[18] This was very likely true. However, the continued growth of all three in the last decade before the American Revolution, when deflationary monetary policies were forced on the colony, shows that market forces were at work that transcended the supplies of paper money. (Since sterling bills of exchange generally circulated as easily as any money, expanded drawing facilities created by larger crops or higher prices and easier British terms may have more than compensated for the declining supply of local paper money.)

The granting by British merchants of ever more extensive credit to the planters and traders of Virginia, Maryland, and the more southerly colonies thus appears quite reasonable, given the increasing wealth and income of the plantation colonies. But where did these metropolitan merchants obtain the resources to support this ever more generous credit? To understand the ability of British firms to sustain such credit, we must understand their ability to mobilize resources—through their own capital, through the reinvestment of earnings, through long-term borrowing on bond, through short-term borrowing from banks, and through the fullest utilization of commercial credit from their suppliers. These various facets of resource mobilization will be explored in the next four chapters.

3

Capitalization of Merchant Firms

THUS FAR, we have been dealing with phenomena familiar in hazy outline if not in detail. We must now turn to some more specific questions of current scholarly interest. First of all, where did the capital come from that provided the £2 million to £4 million advanced to the planters and traders of the tobacco colonies? Some modern historians seem to have assumed automatically, perhaps after reading Jefferson, that (as in populist mythology) all merchants had bottomless pockets from which to press corrupting credit upon the ever innocent planter. In fact, there were not very many really wealthy men in the tobacco trade, even in London—wealthy, that is, by the standards of the contemporary London grandees in the Mediterranean trades, the West Indies trade, the directorates of the three great moneyed companies, and the like.

The seventeenth century produced only two persistent fortunes in the trade, that of Maurice Thompson in the middle decades of the century (whose son became Baron Haversham), and in the later decades that of the Jeffreys, which passed ultimately to the earls and marquesses of Camden. (Sir Jeffrey Jeffreys was reportedly worth £300,000.)[1] In the third of a century following the death of Sir Jeffrey Jeffreys in 1707, there were really only two substantial if exaggerated family fortunes conspicuous in the trade, that of the Perrys in the Virginia trade and of the Hydes in the Maryland trade: both houses went under in the 1740s with great debts still owed them in America. (It was alleged at the time of the Excise Affair of 1733 that even Perry's stock-in-trade was only £20,000.)[2]

On the eve of the Revolution it was reported that there were only two houses in London so affluent as to be set apart from other houses in the trade: those of the Quakers Osgood Hanbury and Silvanus Grove.[3] Grove was a director and ultimately subgovernor of the London Assurance; but the Hanburys left a more permanent mark on British commercial life in the next century in the chemists Allen & Hanburys, the brewers Truman, Hanbury & Buxton, and in Lloyds Bank, whose London progenitor was founded in 1770 as Hanbury, Taylor, Lloyd & Bowman.[4] John Hanbury, the founder of the firm, who died in 1758, was probably worth well over £100,000; quite apart from what he left to his son Osgood, he had settled £30,000 in his lifetime upon his daughter Anna (Mrs. Thomas Barnard).[5] His solidity was recognized by the government when he was made principal contractor for monetary remittances to North America at the start of the Seven Years' War. No firm of "tobacco lords" in Glasgow reached the eminence or continuity of the Hanburys, whose original merchant firm persisted from the 1720s till about 1811. The three significant Glasgow fortunes that survived the American Revolution (Glassford, Cuninghame, and Speirs) all emerged only in the fifteen years preceding the Revolution and were saved from annihilation in the war only by speculative nerve and the tenfold increase in tobacco prices between 1775 and 1783.[6]

The characteristic fortunes engaged in the London trade were by contrast relatively modest. A respectable merchant, Perient Trott, left a personal estate of under £2,000 in 1679. One of the most prominent firms at the turn of the century was that of John Cary & Company. When Cary died in 1701, his inventory revealed an estate of just under £30,000 with only £7,500 invested in the capital of his merchant house. As senior partner his share was probably around 50 percent, suggesting a total "stock" or risk capital for the firm of £15,000 or £20,000 at most.[7] This should be thought of as something of a ceiling, for Carys were then the largest exporters of tobacco from England, and probably close to being the largest house in the Virginia trade after Jeffreys and Perrys.[8] Following the death in 1716 of John Cary's son Thomas, reputed to be relatively wealthy, the firm was continued on a narrower bottom by a succession of partners, including George Hatley, Thomas Flowerdewe, and John Norton.[9] In Norton's time, on the eve of the Revolution, the total risk capital of the firm was only £6,000. Yet his was one of the more respectable consignment houses in London.[10] Not much larger was the firm of James Buchanan, one of the elected members of the committee of Virginia merchants of London. When Buchanan died in 1758, his share of the capital of his firm (which became Hyndman & Lancaster) was also £6,000.[11] It is doubtful if the whole capital of the firm could have been much over £10,000. When Christopher Court, a Maryland merchant, called in his creditors in 1773, his book assets totaled £59,000 and his liabilities £52,000, leaving a nominal balance of only £7,000. Since in those difficult times something extra would have had to be allowed for bad and dubious debts, Joshua Johnson considered that Court had "no Capital" at all.[12] When Johnson himself went over to London as London resident partner of an Annapolis firm, he took with him only £3,000.[13] Since the firm had other assets in Maryland, its true net worth was perhaps double that. By 1776, this had risen to something in the vicinity of £16,000.[14]

There does not appear to be anything anomalous in these relatively modest London capitalizations. The distinguished Russia merchant, Sir Benjamin Ayloffe, left a personal estate of only £8,055 in 1722. The long-established Coutts firm of London and Edinburgh was taken over in the 1760s by new partners including Robert Herries, Sir William Forbes, and James Hunter Blair. It was an influential firm trading primarily to Spain and Italy; in 1771 Herries obtained for it the buying agency of the French tobacco monopoly. Nevertheless its capitalization in 1768 was only £9,800 (£4,400 for the London house of Herries & Company and £5,400 for Edinburgh). Since the policy was to distribute the substantial profits earned as dividends, this total had increased to only £12,300 by 1775 (£6,300 London and £6,000 Edinburgh). Herries also started an additional firm, the London Exchange Banking Company, St. James's Street, with a capitalization of only £3,600.[15]

If our information on the capital structure of the London trade is so sparse as to be only tantalizing, our data for Glasgow are considerably fuller and richer. While most London firms were conducted by single individuals or by small partnerships of two or three individuals, in Glasgow the scarcity of capital made it necessary to draw upon a wider circle of investors to obtain the capital necessary to fund even a small concern in the Virginia trade. Facilitated by the more flexible Scottish partnership law, these arrangements also made it possible for acting and sleeping partners to divide their risks among many firms. (Provost Andrew Cochrane was a partner in five active firms, about 1775.) The normal house in Glasgow contained from four to ten or twelve partners, with five or six perhaps being typical.[16] Thus, firms could be put together with capital in the vicinity of £10,000, though no partner put up more than £2,500 and some put up much less. These large partnerships had some features of the later private joint-stock company. The articles of partnership specified both forms of organization and procedure. Regular minute or sederunt books were kept, and decisions properly entered therein were binding on all the partners. However, Glasgow merchant partnerships did not have such important advantages of incorporation as limited liability or unrestricted transferability of shares.

In the "American" claims in the Public Record Office, in the Registers of Deeds attached to the Burgh and Commissary courts of Glasgow, and elsewhere I have located accounts, articles of copartnery, or other valuations of forty-two Glasgow firms trading to the Chesapeake after 1740. By taking no more than two valuations for any one firm, I obtained fifty-three citations of capital distributed as follows:

Capital	Citations	1740–1763	1764–1789
Under £10,000	16	7	9
£10,000–20,000	22	7	15
Over £20,000	15	3	12

Even though the "average" Glasgow firm had a capital stock of between £10,000 and £20,000, the overall range was rather extreme, from £1,500 to more than £150,000! Although a purely retail shop could be opened in the Chesapeake with only one or two hundred pounds' capital, anything called a "store" making returns in tobacco required a "stock" of nearly £3,000. The one firm with a capital of only £1,500 had its sole store on the eastern shore away from the tobacco-growing regions. Three firms with stocks of £3,000 to £4,000 appear to have each operated one store only. The larger capital stocks permitted formation of the characteristic chains of stores, with roughly one store for every three or four thousand pounds' worth of stock, though some firms chose to operate larger but fewer stores.[17]

With the growth of the trade from the pre-1763 to the post-1763 generation, the size of firms obviously increased. Even so, the size of firms in the 1740–1763 generation (shown in the tabulation), should not be thought of as typical of those in earlier decades of the century. In 1713, probably the largest Glasgow firm in the American trade had a capital of only £7,163.[18] The great expansion during the century in average firm size came primarily through the reinvestment of earnings rather than through the attraction of outside capital, though the latter did occur. The "tobacco lords" of Glasgow had no choice but to plow back their profits, for these were to a great extent book profits that were extremely difficult to realize in the short run. Goods sent out to the Chesapeake could be sold wholesale for cash or early payment at markups or sterling "advances" of from 25 percent to as little as 10 or 15 percent. Most, however, were sold at retail on long credit with advances of up to 80 percent sterling.[19] Though sums owing a firm mounted very rapidly, realization was a much slower process. John Glassford estimated in 1766 that returns were generally about four years in coming home. He may have been a bit pessimistic, but the records are filled with debts of much longer standing. To protect themselves against the illusions of unrealizable paper profits, Glasgow's Chesapeake firms adopted certain understandable precautions. In making up their annual balances, not only were bad debts valued at nil and doubtful debts at 50 percent, but for good measure an extra 15 to 20 percent was knocked off the reduced total of good and doubtful debts (to cover, among other things, interest and costs of collection). Further, almost all firms had rules restricting the payment of dividends from profits except when winding up. In the normal operation of the firm, only 5 percent interest was paid on the capital credited to the partners. All other profits (when made) were distributed on the books as capital appreciation of the shares of the partners. This combination of financial self-discipline and accounting generosity could lead to a very rapid increase in the ostensible capital of a firm.

Alexander Speirs lived in Virginia in the 1740s as representative of the important Buchanan firm of Glasgow. In 1749, he returned to Scotland and became a partner in the substantial Virginia firm of Buchanan, Speirs & Company, which after the death of Archibald Buchanan of Silverbank in 1761 became Speirs, Bowman & Company. When a new partnership contract was drawn up in 1754, the capital was given as £16,200. This may have understated matters slightly (as there was no change of partners then), for only seven years later, at Archibald Buchanan's death, arbitrators valued his (Buchanan's) 30/162 share at £13,750, making the net worth of the whole firm £74,250.[20] A subsequent partnership contract of June 1773 put the capital at £152,280, making Speirs & Company the largest firm in the trade (as it was also the largest importer of tobacco). The capital of Speirs' parallel Maryland firm, Speirs, Mackie & Company, later Speirs, French & Company, increased from £6,240 in 1765 to £27,577 in 1771 and £55,872 in 1779.[21] Similar if not as striking growth can be found among lesser firms in Glasgow. Buchanan, Hastie & Company seems to have had a capital of about £10,000 to £10,500 in 1770–1772 and a book stock of £23,014 in 1774;[22] John Alston & Company had an avowed stock of £12,000 in 1767, while its successor, Alston, Young & Company, was worth £26,850 on paper in 1775.[23]

Alexander Speirs was by no means the only great Glasgow entrepreneur whose undertakings reached capitalizations near or above £100,000. Comparable levels were reached by the firms of those other members of the local "big three," William Cuninghame and John Glassford. Like Speirs, Cuninghame had served in Virginia as a factor in the 1740s. Just as Speirs advanced through alliance with the old Glasgow money of the Buchanans, so William Cuninghame returned to Glasgow to head a firm incorporating the preexisting wealth of Provost Andrew Cochrane and of the Murdochs and Bogles. His Virginia house (William Cuninghame & Company) had a capitalization of £79,200 in 1773; his Maryland firm in his brother's name (Alexander Cuninghame & Company, later Cuninghame, Findlay & Company) had had a capitalization of £15,000 by its articles of 1769, though most of this was lost through mismanagement at the American end in the crisis year 1772.[24] John Glassford came into the trade by quite a different route. We first meet him in the 1740s as a partner in the firm of Ingram & Glassford, warehousemen, who supplied the merchants of Glasgow with the textiles needed for the export trade. While his firm integrated backward by investment in manfacture, starting the pioneer inkle (linen-tape) manufacture in the west of Scotland,[25] Glassford integrated forward by extensive investment in shipping and trading concerns. At the time of the Seven Years' War, he was supposed to have had interests in twenty-five ships.[26] We do not know the capital of his main house, the Potomac (Maryland and Virginia) concern of John Glassford & Company, nor of his north Virginia (Rappahannock) firm, Glassford, Henderson & Company, but that of the former was probably in the vicinity of £50,000 in 1770. His firm trading in southern Virginia (styled Glassford, Gordon, Monteath & Company in Scotland and Neil Jamieson & Company in Virginia) provided for a stock of £24,000 in its articles of 1771;[27] and his upper James River firm Henderson, McCall & Company (formerly George Kippen & Company) had a capital of £35,000 about the same time.[28] Speirs, Cuninghame, and Glassford, each having companies with a combined capitalization near or over £100,000, were in a class by themselves, for such clusters of companies were rare, and few individual firms in Glasgow's Chesapeake trade ever had stocks exceeding £30,000.[29]

Thus, even though there were no *individual* fortunes in Glasgow before 1776 comparable to those of the greatest London grandees (between £100,000 and £300,000), the big Glasgow partnerships reached levels of capitalization that far overshadowed almost anything imaginable in the London tobacco trade. Although the wealthier planters and rentiers of Virginia and Maryland, with fortunes in the £10,000 to £80,000 range,[30] could address London commission houses somewhat condescendingly, and younger brothers like William Lee of Virginia could hope to move to London and compete with them, Speirs, Cuninghame, and Glassford belonged to quite a different world. In Scotland, only the Carron ironworks, with a capitalization in 1773 of £130,000, was at all comparable among private companies.[31] In Glasgow, the only activities remotely comparable were the sugar works, with stocks of £7,000 to £14,000, and the tanneries with capital in the £8,000 to £12,000 range.[32] Most of the local linen manufacturing firms I have found any trace of before 1770 had stocks under £1,000, but my information here is quite sparse. One Glasgow merchant firm with interests in linen manufacture had a capital of £8,000 in 1765, and linen and cotton printing firms there between 1759 and 1773 had capitals of £4,000–£8,400.[33] Since most of the partners in the sugar works and other large manufacturing firms in and near Glasgow were Chesapeake and West India merchants, the financial preeminence of such traders in local society remained unchallenged.

Much less is known about the capital of firms in

the English outports. For Whitehaven nothing at all is known except that Walter Lutwidge, thought to be the richest merchant there, had a personal fortune of £30,000 about 1740.[34] Information about Chesapeake houses in Liverpool is almost as thin, perhaps because virtuous Victorian descendants destroyed most records touching on their ancestors' slave-trading activities. We do know that when Sir Ellis Cunliffe, head of the greatest Chesapeake trading firm in the port, died in 1767, he left a personal estate (exclusive of real estate) of about £65,000. Since his brother Robert had also inherited, it is likely that their father Foster Cunliffe's personal estate by itself had exceeded £100,000 when he died in 1758. As the Cunliffes were the greatest outport traders to the Chesapeake (particularly to Maryland) at the middle of the century, these figures should not be regarded as typical but rather as setting an upper limit.[35]

Perhaps more representative and certainly more informative are the annual accounts of John Tarleton (1718–1773), a Liverpool merchant active as an underwriter and trader primarily to the West Indies but also to Africa (the slave trade) and North America (to Philadelphia and New York). In addition, like the Cunliffes, Tarleton had local interests in sugar refining. Table 5 shows that the plowing back of trading profits, made possible by relatively modest living expenses, led to the accumulation of a very substantial fortune by Tarleton and ultimately to the founding of a landed family. This was aided by his considerable good fortune in investing in privateers during the Seven Years' War.[36]

Quakers, on the other hand, were unlikely to invest in privateers, but for them too mercantile acu-

Table 5. *The estate of John Tarleton of Liverpool, 1749–1773.*

Date	Stock-in-trade	Total fortune	Cash
18 Mar. 1748/9	£4,275	£6,105	—
6 Feb. 1749/50	4,653	7,798	—
4 May 1752	6,569	9,862	£496
13 June 1754	11,493	12,700	941
— May 1755	11,697	12,900	—
26 Apr. 1758	—	22,940	2,508
24 Mar. 1759	—	28,590	—
16 May 1760	—	32,260	8,426
21 May 1761	—	40,017	5,104
24 June 1762	—	45,297	7,274
1 June 1763	—	53,010	11,097
2 May 1764	54,729	57,000	11,833
31 Mar. 1766	60,650	62,500	5,148
31 Mar. 1767	62,387	63,219	—
30 Apr. 1768	62,682	63,300	—
29 Apr. 1769	—	64,038	1,783
30 Apr. 1770	—	69,544	2,257
30 Apr. 1771	—	73,218	—
30 Apr. 1772	—	75,224	—
30 Apr. 1773	—	79,356	—

Source: Liverpool RO, 920 Tar 2/1–17, 2/18/2, 2/19/1–3, 2/20/1–2, 2/21A,B.

men, controlled living expenses, the reinvestment of savings, and long life could lead to the most impressive accumulations of personal fortunes and trading capital. Since Quaker families seem to have saved their papers somewhat more often than others we have several interesting examples of their good management. Edward Harford, Jr., a second- or third-generation Quaker merchant of Bristol, trading to Virginia, was related to the Lloyds and Pembertons of Birmingham, for whom he sometimes handled ironmongery exports to America on commission, but his primary business before 1775 was that of a tobacco commission merchant. In the late 1740s he appears to have taken over a small Virginia trade from his father; and when his father died in 1779, Edward Jr. inherited over £19,000. Before that, however, his fortune was formed by the slow accumulation and reinvestment of profits (table 6), an accumulation unassisted by a Tarleton's gains from privateers and slave trading or any extraordinary wartime windfalls.[37]

In London other Quakers prospered in wartime even while avoiding unacceptable traffics. John Eliot of London (1683–1762) had inherited land and tin interests in Cornwall and was active as a merchant trading to the Mediterranean and less regularly to the West Indies. However, his principal income came from insurance underwriting. When his surviving detailed accounts commence in 1722, he had a net personal estate of £11,230.2.7; by 1740 his total estate was £39,596 (including £7,402 in real estate); at his death in 1762 he was worth £97,989. After 1740, the principal growth of his estate came from increased insurance earnings in wartime, though he also profited from the increase in the value of public stocks at the end of the war in 1748. For forty years, his accounts show his very tight control over household and personal expenses. These expenses, which were £500 a year in the early 1720s, had no more than doubled by the end of his life even though his estate had probably increased at least fivefold. Eliot's only obvious luxuries were his carriages and horses, which usually cost him between £100 and £150 per annum.[38]

Much the same pattern can be found in the accounts of a more conspicuous Quaker, Samuel Hoare, the ancestor of Sir Samuel Hoare, viscount Temple-

Table 6. *The estate of Edward Harford, Jr., of Bristol, 1748–1806.*

Date	Total stock	Household expenses	Stock-in-Trade Date	Amount
Mar. 1748	£7,050	—		
Mar. 1749	7,055	—		
Mar. 1750	7,111	£343		
Mar. 1751	8,250	340		
Mar. 1752	9,040	362		
31 Dec. 1752	9,460	258	30 June 1752	£4,597
31 Dec. 1753	10,090	351	30 Apr. 1753	5,018
31 Dec. 1754	11,675	332	31 May 1754	5,545
31 Dec. 1755	12,270	408	30 June 1755	7,137
31 Dec. 1756	13,080	383	1 Sept. 1756	7,146
31 Dec. 1757	13,680	356	1 July 1757	7,694
31 Dec. 1758	13,250	364	1 Oct. 1758	8,562
31 Dec. 1759	14,200	385	31 Dec. 1759	7,934
31 Dec. 1760	15,450	378	31 Dec. 1760	9,357
31 Dec. 1761	15,800	341	30 Nov. 1761	8,683
31 Dec. 1762	16,900	375	31 Dec. 1762	9,915
31 Dec. 1763	18,000	434	31 Dec. 1763	11,293
31 Dec. 1764	18,700	393	31 Dec. 1764	11,820
31 Dec. 1765	19,375	374	31 Dec. 1765	12,472
31 Dec. 1766	20,350	427	31 Dec. 1766	12,420
31 Dec. 1767	21,250	425	31 Dec. 1767	13,359
31 Dec. 1768	22,590	494	31 Dec. 1768	14,171
1769–1779	—	—		
1 Jan. 1780	43,093	—		
31 Dec. 1780	42,276	—		
31 Dec. 1781	43,602	—		
31 Dec. 1782	65,868[a]	—		
31 Dec. 1783	65,641	—		
31 Dec. 1784	69,820	—		
31 Dec. 1785	70,498	—		
31 Dec. 1786	70,483	—		
31 Dec. 1806	154,511[b]	—		

Source: Bristol AO, Harford Family Papers, bdls. VIII/1a (personal ledger of E. Harford, Jr.), VII/2a (ledger C), and VIII/9 (estate papers, 1806).

a. Including more than £19,000 from his father's estate.

b. Estate at death.

wood. Born in 1716 into a Quaker family established in County Cork since Cromwell's time, he was the son of Joseph Hoare, a county landowner and banker-merchant in the city of Cork. Samuel, who also became a small merchant in Cork, must have increased his inheritance after the death of his older brother Joseph in 1740, and by 1743 he appears to have been worth about £11,510 sterling (£6,860 in Irish lands and £4,650 in personalty). In 1744 he married Grizell, daughter of Jonathan Gurnell of London, who brought him a dowry of £4,000. At the same time he moved to London and acquired for £8,000 a one-third interest in her father's firm, Jonathan Gurnell & Company. With the death of both her father and brother he became a principal partner in the firm, successively known as Gurnell & Hoare; Gurnell, Hoare & Harman; and (after his retirement) Harman, Hoare & Company. The firm appears to have been active in the Irish, Portuguese, and Dutch trades, but it also had Pennsylvania connections. In 1768, acting for its Amsterdam correspondents, Hope & Company, it was briefly the buying agent in London for the French tobacco monopoly. (It was also the London correspondent of the French court banker, Jean-Joseph de la Borde.)

Despite membership in this prestigious firm, Samuel Hoare lived relatively modestly at first. Between 1749 and 1763 his annual living expenses averaged £785, roughly equivalent to Eliot's level. However, he too seems to have prospered greatly during the Seven Years' War, and in 1764 he commenced a grander style of life, perhaps reflecting both the greater prosperity of his firm and his children's approach to marriageable age. His living expenses were to average £1,434 in 1764–1778 and £1,891 in 1778–1790. However, such expenses were covered by his receipts from rents and interest (including interest on "surplus capital" lent to the firm). The profits from his mercantile business were almost entirely saved and reinvested. Thus, his net worth was to increase from the £11,510 of 1743 to over £69,000 in 1775 and—despite his retirement—to £82,651 in 1795. This accumulation was aided by his receipt of £9,075 in dowry and inheritances (mostly from his wife's family) between 1744 and 1772; on the other side of the ledger, however, he paid out £28,150 between 1769 and 1790 in dowries and portions to his children. If his children's portions are added to his own estate, it would seem that saving and reinvesting profits had increased his possessions from about £11,500 in 1743 to almost ten times as much in 1795, exclusive of any appreciation in the value of his real estate.[39] This was a more rapid rate of growth than that of the capital of his firm, which appears to have risen from £24,000 in 1744–1747 to about £63,000 in 1767 and £100,000 in 1774.[40]

The accounts of Tarleton and the three Quakers are interesting for what they reveal about the mechanics of the reinvestment of earnings and the resulting steady accretion of fortunes, but they should not be regarded as typical. Few contemporary overseas merchants had the good judgment, the good health, and perhaps the good luck of these four founders of lasting family fortunes; and most ended up with much less to show for their pains and anxieties. Most too probably started out with less. Tarleton, Harford, Eliot, and Hoare ended up with estates more than tenfold those with which they had started, but all four seem to have begun with respectable competencies from their families. For those who started out with less the going was usually much more arduous, for of course the first £5,000 was, as ever, the hardest to come by.

The minimum needed to set up as an overseas merchant varied from trade to trade. As already noted, it was difficult to start out in the Atlantic trades without several thousands of pounds unless one could join a Glasgow firm or some other strong partnership. In trades closer to home, starts could be made with much more modest competencies. William Kennaway of Exeter, a merchant exporting cloth to Iberia and Italy and importing wine, has left annual accounts of his estate from 1746 until his death in 1793. These show the net worth of his firm (first himself alone and then a partnership with his son) increasing from £529 in August 1746 to £43,249 in August 1793.[41] The growth rate was probably exceptional; the range of capitalization seems consistent with that of other Exeter cloth exporters, though one could not get very far in the America trades with an initial capital of only £500.[42]

Even in cloth much greater fortunes could be made by those prepared to risk the America trades. The Elams started out as tobacconists in Leeds, presumably buying their tobacco from importers in the ports. Seeing the possibilities of developing direct contact with the Chespeake, they eventually created a business exporting West Riding cloth from Hull to Virginia, and returning tobacco. When Emmanuel Elam died in 1793 he was reportedly worth over £200,000. Even if he had been worth only one-quarter as much in 1775, he would have been quite near the top in either the Virginia trade or the West Riding woolen trade. In the latter, the largest firm (William

Milner) had a capital of £25,000 in 1737, while a medium-sized export firm (Ibbetson & Koster) had a capital of £9,500 that rose to £12,300 by 1760. After 1783, capitalizations were noticeably larger in Leeds, and one new firm started with over £40,000—but still the Elam level was unmatched.[43]

Quite comparable with the prerevolutionary levels found in Leeds was the fortune of William Russell of Birmingham (1740–1818), a general merchant with wide interests including the Baltic and North America trades and ironworks in Maryland (the Principio Company). His personal fortune rose from £13,212 in 1774 to over £25,000 after 1781 and to £45,000 in the 1790s. He had been interested, among other things, in a general merchant house with American interests—Smith, Son & Russell—which was wound up about 1775, when his principal interest shifted to the firm of Finch & Russell, importing iron and linen from the Baltic and exporting Birmingham ware to both the Baltic and North America. Its capital rose from £14,000 in 1775 to about £24,000 in 1777; in 1778 it became Finch, Russell & Wright with a capital of £30,000, only to be wound up after the war and replaced by the more modest firm of Russell, Russell & Smith with a capital of £15,000.[44]

The pre-1775 Leeds figures also seem consistent with the capitalization figures for the Gurneys of Norwich. With changing partners the capitalization of their mercantile firm rose from £12,000 in 1741 (Joseph & John Gurney) to £70,000 in 1767–1769 (John, Samuel & Richard Gurney). This firm was then wound up and the succeeding firm of Richard & John Gurney, later Gurney & Bland, experienced a slow rise in capital from £40,000 in 1771 to £60,000 in 1780. The

Gurneys were engaged primarily in the importation of Irish yarn and its sale to the Norwich cloth trade; they avoided the substantial American involvements of their Quaker connections the Barclays and Hanburys, but by the 1780s they were involved slightly in the export of East Anglian cloth to Iberia. Nevertheless, it is useful to be reminded that capitalization in such relatively internal trades could reach levels that overshadowed all but the largest transatlantic firms.[45]

In short, the characteristic pattern for a firm trading to the Chesapeake or elsewhere in America before 1775 seems to have been to start with capital in the range of £5,000–£10,000, slightly larger perhaps for some big Glasgow partnerships or a very few second-generation English firms. The more detailed Glasgow data imply that capitalizations below £3,000 were all but impossible, though the Exeter information suggests that in a purely European trade where one did not have to maintain ships, smaller capitalizations were feasible. From this base, good fortune, good health, and the constant reinvestment of profits might make possible the gradual accumulations of much larger trading stocks, tenfold increases in one lifetime being not unknown. The Glasgow evidence places the median firm at between £10,000 and £20,000; other places and trades were probably not far from this.[46] The rate of capital accumulation appears to have accelerated after 1783, particularly in the inflationary war years after 1793, and turn-of-the-century fortunes, such as Emmanuel Elam's reported £200,000 or Edward Harford's £154,000, would have been almost unknown before 1776 (though as noted, Foster Cunliffe and John Hanbury left something near £100,000 in 1758).

From all this highly disparate data, is it possible to derive any aggregates on merchants' trading capital? When we compare some of our bits and pieces on trading capital with what is known about the imports of firms, a rather mixed picture emerges. The data on John Norton & Sons and on Wallace, Davidson & Johnson suggest that a London commission firm in 1775 needed between £7.10.0 and £8.0.0 stock (or net working capital) for every hogshead of tobacco imported. For Glasgow, however, the 1775 data seem to suggest anywhere from £11 to £25 or higher of stock per hogshead imported, and Speirs was among the least efficient of the major firms. However, it is clear from other sources that Speirs was heavily involved in the grain trade as well as the tobacco trade in the Chesapeake so that the tobacco measurement may not be meaningful. In addition, Glasgow imports may not be a full measurement of Glasgow activity since some tobacco purchased by Clyde firms in the Chesapeake was shipped to London. If, for Great Britain as a whole, we assume an average of £10 capital or stock for each hogshead imported on the eve of the Revolution, we imply that the 100,000 hogsheads per annum imported into Britain from the Chesapeake in 1771–1775 required a combined capital of about £1 million. If all the trades to North America, the West Indies, and Africa had approximately the same capital requirements as the tobacco trade, the total stock invested in those trades would have been in the vicinity of £4.5 million.[47]

Before leaving the problem of the capital needs of merchant houses, we must remember one important but highly variable demand on capital, namely shipping. It was possible to go into some trades without

providing one's own shipping, particularly when that trade consisted primarily in exporting (or even importing) valuable products of small bulk, such as cloth. However, no one could engage in the importation of such bulky products as timber, tar, hemp, iron—or the classic American products, sugar and tobacco—without assuring a fair proportion of his shipping space in advance. This might mean chartering all or part of a ship for one voyage only, or buying or building one's own vessel. In the generation or so before the Revolution, freight rates in the Chesapeake trade in peacetime for small shipments were commonly £8 sterling per ton (four hogsheads) from Virginia, and between £7.0.0 and £7.10.0 from Maryland.[48] Freight of about £2 per hogshead was a stiff charge when ordinary tobacco usually netted less than £5 per hogshead after the deduction of all charges and the commission. The same ships went outward bound for the most part in ballast and took partial cargoes of manufactures and the like for freights of only 2.5 percent of value; such freights could contribute only a small share of a ship's round-trip earnings. The high freights homeward and the uncertainty of finding space for large shipments as needed induced most firms in the West India or Chesapeake trade to acquire their own vessels or charter them in entirety to obtain surer service and better rates.[49] Either method created pressure on the firm's capital resources, liquidity, and cash flow.

In the Chesapeake some vessels might be chartered on the spot from local builders, who expected to sell the vessels in Britain after one voyage there.[50] Far more common for the Chesapeake as for the West India trade was chartering in Britain. This presupposed the existence of a fairly large fleet of vessels (hundreds or even thousands) available for charter as needed. Ralph Davis's work on the shipping industry has shown that returns to owners were not exceptionally high on vessels available for charter.[51] Why then did people invest in them? Was it just that they could obtain 1 or 2 percent more per annum than the 4 percent or so available from mortgages or government stock in the middle decades of the century? This question requires close attention because through investment in shipping small investors not themselves merchants made millions in resources available to the mercantile sector.

Unfortunately, very few good accounts of ship ownership and management have survived. In addition to those cited by Davis, attention should be called to a remarkable exhibit in the Chancery Petty Bag Office: the ledgers, journals, letterbooks, and other records of George Tarbutt (& Sons), West India merchants of London, 1793–1800. In addition to recording a normal West India commission business, these accounts cover Tarbutts' activities as part owners and managers (ship's husband) of several vessels in the West India trade. These reveal that Tarbutts were the largest owners of each of the vessels managed, usually holding about $\frac{5}{16}$ or $\frac{6}{16}$ of each. Other big shareholders were their Jamaican mercantile correspondents, Charles and William Bryan and John and Jacob Neufville. The related Bryans and Neufvilles between them generally held one-fourth of each ship. The remaining shares were commonly held in units of $\frac{1}{16}$ or $\frac{2}{16}$ by the captain and by small investors in London who can usually be identified in Tarbutts' own books as shipchandlers, ropemakers, sailmakers, and the like. Their interest in a ship gave them an apparently unchallengeable claim to its supply business. Arthur Shakespear, ropemaker, had a $\frac{1}{16}$ share in four out of five of Tarbutts' ships and obtained the rope business of each; in the fifth (the *Windsor Castle*), another ropemaker, Edward Gale, was part owner and accordingly got its supply business. Similarly, John & James Mangles, ship chandlers, obtained the chandlery business for the *Windsor Castle*, in which they held a $\frac{1}{16}$ share, but their rivals Ede & Allen (later Nathaniel Allen & Son) got the chandlery business for the *Amity Hall* and *Monmouth*, in which they held sixteenths. The sailmaker Dorothy Turner (later in partnership with her son Charles) procured the appropriate contracts for these three vessels, in which she held sixteenths. A ship's carpenter, John Dudman, held $\frac{2}{16}$ in what appear to have been two successive ships named *John* and likewise received their carpentry business.[52]

Seen in this light, taking shares in ships was not simply a form of purely speculative investment. Merchants in Britain, merchants in America, ship captains, ship suppliers, all persons with definite needs for shipping services or shipping business, took shares in ships to help guarantee access to the services or patronage they needed. The Tarbutt accounts are perhaps unique among surviving records in their detail. However, it is unlikely that they were unique in their representation of business practices.[53]

In Whitehaven, there was a rather special shipping problem in that local vessels were commonly used for the Virginia trade only six months of the year (February–July) and were employed in carrying local coal to Ireland during the other six months. It was important to both the Chesapeake interest and the coal interest to make sure that ships would be available when needed. Thus, we find the great local coal owner Sir James Lowther, Bart., and his father, Sir John, taking small shares in many ships to increase the coal-carrying capacity of the port when needed.[54] With the coal interest thus engaged, the Chesapeake interest could not slumber. An inquest in 1763 into the estate of Peter How, a great Whitehaven tobacco merchant and sometime buying agent for the French monopoly, shows that he held shares in twenty-four vessels, mostly from one-sixteenth to one-eighth each.[55] It would appear that such small investments were enough to guarantee that shipping would be available for How's purposes when needed.

Whether they were London ship chandlers looking for patronage or Cumberland coal owners looking for carrying capacity, persons outside the America trade were prepared to invest in shipping for that trade. This meant that firms in the trade were relieved of part of the obligation of providing capital resources and could stretch their limited funds farther than they otherwise would have been able to do.

4

Borrowing on Bond

E VEN CAPITAL AMOUNTS of the Glasgow
levels were by themselves quite inadequate
for the Chesapeake trade, given its tendency to sink
everything into long credits. To supplement their own
resources, most merchant houses seem to have borrowed extensively on bond for the medium or long
term. In London, John Norton & Company, with a
capital of £6,000, had £7,500 borrowed from outside
in 1773 in addition to personal advances made by the
senior partner; and Norton raised the £7,500 from
only five individuals.[1] Following the panic of 1772,
the London Scottish firm of William & Robert Molleson (the largest in the London trade in 1775) was
reported as able to borrow £10,000 on short order
from friends and relations.[2] Even more impressive, the
London Scottish firm of Robert & Robert Bogle & Scott
had just before that borrowed £5,000 on bond from a
single rentier described as a "Schoolbred man of great
fortune in England."[3]

There was nothing unusual about such activity,
for there had long been an active bond market in

London. A bond of indebtedness may be described as a deed of obligation from debtor to creditor signed by at least two persons (frequently the debtor and a surety) and containing a penalty for nonpayment, which in England was double the actual debt. In the 1660s the merchant-financier John Banks both borrowed on bond (up to £1,200 at a time) from his Kentish neighbors at 5 percent and lent to others on bond (presumably at a higher rate of interest). He was able to get through the crisis of the Stop of the Exchequer in 1672 only by his ability to raise larger sums on bond quickly, including £3,000 from one source. After retiring from trade in the 1680s he lent more of his own funds out on bond. Other later examples can be given: a small wine importer (Joseph Bowles) at his death in 1701 owed £1,100 on four bonds of between £100 and £400 each; and a not much larger merchant (John Hall) trading to Spain and the West Indies died in 1703 owing £1,400 on two long-standing bonds. A Baltic merchant (Henry Phill) in 1706 owed £6,500 in bonds (of £100 to £1,500 each) to nine different persons, and, half a century later in 1757, a small merchant trading to Portugal was able to borrow £3,000 on bond from a prominent barrister. When the great Africa and West India merchant Humphrey Morice died in 1731, he owed £16,000 on bonds and other specialties. He had formerly borrowed £26,500 on bond from his kinsman Sir William Morice.[4]

There is also some evidence of the London bond market from the side of the lenders. Sir William Turner, knight, an alderman of London and retired draper, left in 1693 personal effects of over £50,000, mostly in bonds, mortgages, and company shares. His bonds alone came to £27,692. Many of these were nonmercantile but others were clearly commercial, including £3,990 from the Royal Africa Company, £1,133 from the Hudson's Bay Company, £1,370 from Richard Thompson & Company, and £500 owed by William Atwill & Company. The inventory (1705) of the estate of Simon Cole, a wine merchant of the parish of St. Margaret Lothbury, London, shows that he was acting as agent for Josias Calmady, Esq., a Devon landowner, for whom he had placed £2,000 in three big bonds. The 1725 inventory of the estate of Manasses Whitehead of the parish of St. Andrew Undershaft, London, an active wine and cloth merchant, totaled £120,253 and included sixty bonds, twenty-two of which were over £100.[5] When David Barclay, a substantial but semiretired London linen merchant and banker, died in 1809, he left a personal estate of between £39,000 and £43,000, of which £29,000 was in bonds and £3,700 in bills and notes.[6]

The same pattern of heavy lending and borrowing on bond can be found in the English outports. Perhaps the clearest picture of the use of bonds by a Virginia merchant can be seen in the papers of John King of Bristol. Although his account books have not survived, his executor (Thomas Liston) appears to have preserved all the bonds outstanding at the time of King's death on 29 November 1734. King was a Virginia merchant importing about 250,000 pounds of tobacco yearly. In addition he was, from at least 1724 on, interested with Lyonel Lyde, John Lewis, Jeremy Innys, Thomas Longman, and William Donne, also merchants of Bristol, in the BC Company, proprietors of ironworks in northern Virginia, one of the earliest such operations in that province. And occasionally he took a flier with some other Bristol merchants in side ventures in the corn trade.

King's bonds reflect his various ventures. For his tobacco imports, there were customs bonds for the duties, ranging up to £2,000 in value. Most of these were cosigned by his brother-in-law Thomas Liston, Esq., of Iron Acton (Gloucestershire), or by the well-to-do Bristol linendraper Paul Fisher, whose customer King undoubtedly was. Other customs bonds were signed by Bristol merchants, Jeremy Innys, Thomas Longman (both King's partners in the ironworks), and Christopher Willoughby.[7] King undoubtedly reciprocated by signing their customs bonds. For ordinary commercial purposes, there was a renewed bond for £1,000 borrowed at 5 percent in 1728 from Ann Hicks, spinster, by John King, his late brother Walter King, Edward Buckler, maltster, and Paul Fisher, for ventures in the corn trade.[8] The largest group of bonds, however, involved borrowing by John King for his own business. We have details of twelve such bonds totaling £4,428.10.0 (exclusive of current interest) and going back to 1726. None had more than one additional signature as surety. The oldest group of bonds, 1726–1732, all for £200–£270, were to women (Anne Smith, Hannah Cole, and Elizabeth Gwyn, all of Bristol, and to Frances Berkeley, spinster, of Stapleton, Gloucestershire). That of 1732 to Gwyn was for 4.5 percent interest; the others were all for 5 percent. These women appear to have been widows and spinsters seeking safe long-term investments for inherited funds. The largest bonds, however, were two of February 1733/4 for £700 and £600, loans to him from John Cox, Edmund Saunders, Cossley Rogers,

and the other partners in the Bristol Crown Fire
Office! These are remarkable both for their size and
their source.[9] Recent work has emphasized that in the
eighteenth century the London insurance companies
were very conservative in their investment policy,
preferring exchequer bills and other government stock
and only very cautiously lending on the security of
their own and other stock or jewels and of some mortgages, but never lending to merchants on bond, bill, or
note secured only by signatures.[10] That a Bristol insurance company should lend to King with only Liston as
surety gives weight to Peter Dickson's point about the
differing investment patterns of the metropolis and
the provinces. Another large bond (£500 at 4.5 percent
in 1731) was from King to Robert Smith, Jeremy Innys, Joseph Brown, and Joseph Iles, all merchants of
Bristol. They were perhaps executors or trustees of an
estate looking for a good long-term investment. The
remaining bonds, all quite recent in date and all at the
full 5 percent, were to men of Bristol who were not
merchants, £300 and £200 to William Thornhill, sur-
geon, £370 to John Vizard, tobacconist, £688.10.0 to
James Cadell, mercer, and £200 to the executors of the
will of Christopher Merryweather, victualler. These
would appear to represent local savings seeking "safe"
local investment at the highest possible interest.[11] Except for the insurance company, those lending to King
on bond were quite similar to lenders on bond
throughout the provinces.

In addition to his individual bonds, King was
cosigner with other partners in £5,400 worth of bonds
of the BC Company, proprietors of the ironworks in
Virginia. His share in this firm was $\frac{4}{36}$ up to 1730 when
Colonel (John?) Tayloe, the firm's manager in Vir-

ginia, was admitted to a $\frac{4}{40}$ share, reducing King's interest to the same amount. All these bonds, dating from 1728 to 1732, were at 4.5 percent interest except one to Richard Gravett, Esq. (a former sheriff of Bristol), at 4 percent, suggesting that the credit rating of the ironworks was about 0.5 percent better than that of King alone. The sources of funds were similar to those tapped by King: two bonds from the Bristol Crown Fire Office (£700 and £600); two from local women (Sarah James, £300, and Anne Wraxall, £600), two from Henry Parson, Esq. (£700 and £600), another from Richard Gravett, Esq. (£600), and one from Henry Walter, Esq., a former mayor (£400), one from the executors of Mr. Joseph Thomas (£600), and another from the executors of Mr. Samuel Bury (£300).[12]

In addition to his bonded debt for customs and for his private and joint ventures, King also owed £1,858.9.0 in seven promissory notes with an average value of about £110 (compared with £369 for his private bonds). A promissory note was less formal than a bond and frequently lacked the second or surety signature. However, King's borrowing on note was quite similar to his borrowing on bond. Apart from a very small promissory note of a family nature, the notes went back to 1728 and were similar to the bonds in interest rates: eight at 5 percent, four at 4.5, and the rest unspecified. Nine, or more than half, represented loans from women, including three (£100, £150, and £200) from Mrs. Elizabeth Addison. One was to Robert Earle, Esq., another former mayor (£250), and one to Abraham Elton (£100), both scions of old Bristol families moving toward rentier status.[13]

John King was also a former mayor and must

have been a very solid and respected member of the Bristol mercantile community to be able to borrow as much as he did. Less established people had difficulty borrowing outside their own family. For example, Mark Harford of Bristol, who had inherited capital of only £1,000 about 1720 and needed £1,666.13.4 for his one-third share in a firm with a capitalization of £5,000, borrowed the balance on bond and note, mostly from members of his family.[14] However, as a merchant's fortune grew, he found it easier and easier to borrow from outside the family. This principle is well represented in the career of John Tarleton of Liverpool, whose accumulation of wealth was described in the last chapter.

There is an old joke about one immigrant attempting to persuade another that America was really the land of promise. "Just think," he said, "twenty five years ago I arrived with nothing; today I owe a million dollars!" There is, of course, a substantial truth beneath the irony: the ability to borrow ever larger sums of money is a measure of one's advancement in the world. When John Tarleton's surviving accounts opened in March 1748/9, he had £5,874 employed in trade: £4,275 of his own stock, £420 on bond from his mother, Bridget Tarleton, £480 on bond from his sister, Ann Tarleton, and only £700 from others.[15] In succeeding accounts, the more his net worth increased, the more money he was able to obtain from others on bond for use in his trade. By 1758, his personal fortune had increased from the £6,105 of 1749 (including the £4,275 in trade) to £22,940; correspondingly, the amounts he owed on bond increased to £4,145, including £1,275 to Robert Milnes, £800 to Sir Roger Bradsheigh, and £400 to George Warrington.[16] After that, his enormous gains from privateering during the war left him with substantial cash balances and he gradually reduced his outstanding bonds except those to his mother and sister. By the mid 1760s he was lending to others on bond. However, shortly before his death he began borrowing again, and his account for 1773 shows what appears to be £5,220 borrowed on bond or note.[17] Tarleton's accounts are in several respects unrepresentative. The considerable wealth he acquired by privateering in the Seven Years' War and the large cash balances that ensued were exceptional. His dependence (when he needed loans) on a few large lenders on bond rather than on a larger number of smaller lenders is more suggestive of the affluence of London than of the relative capital poverty of the provinces. It is, however, possible that some of the companies in which Tarleton was interested borrowed from smaller people on bond, even if he himself did not. There is, for example, a note toward the end of his life that his sugarhouse firm, John Tarleton & Company, owed on bond £3,252 to Tarleton personally, £1,224 to John Backhouse, £161.3.3 to John Preston, and £277.8.10 to the executors of L. Olker.[18]

We learn from other sources that Lancashire had an active local market in mortgages and bonds in units of £200 and less, much of it handled by local attorneys. The instance is cited of the "Preston spinster, Susanna Doughty, who heard that Thomas Ball of Ormskirk, later of Liverpool, attorney, 'was a person very much made use of by several persons for the placing out of their moneys at interest, and that he would be a very proper person to be employed in putting out the money, having the character and reputation of a very careful, substantial honest man.' Some of her money was lent to Richard Norris of Speke, a mayor [and Virginia merchant] of Liverpool."[19]

We have relatively little information about the situation at Whitehaven. Despite Whitehaven's large Chesapeake trade in the 1740s and 1750s, it was a small town and port located in a remote and thinly populated section of the country; and merchants there must have found it relatively difficult to raise additional funds on bonds. In the 1740s Captain Thomas Lutwidge, one of the pioneers in the development of the Whitehaven store trade in the Chesapeake, was having great difficulty raising £2,000 to meet bills of exchange drawn on him by his factors in the Chesapeake. If unable to raise that sum, he would be forced to accept the French buying agents' low prices for superior tobacco that ordinarily would be sold at much higher prices in England or Holland. To avoid this, he proposed an arrangement by which John Spedding, the agent at Whitehaven for Sir James Lowther, principal landlord of the port, would advance him some money in return for accepted bills of exchange payable in London. Sir James sometimes agreed to such arrangements, even taking bills of up to six months' duration, because he had difficulty remitting his rental and coal receipts to London.[20] His successor, Sir James Lowther the younger (1736–1802), the future first earl of Lonsdale, went further and lent money to local merchants on bond. (When Peter How failed in the 1760s, firms in which he was interested were indebted to Sir James Lowther for £6,500 on bond.)[21]

One should not think that this pattern of extensive borrowing on bond was in any way confined to merchants in the North America and West India trades. In fact, a merchant or other trader in purely domestic trade should have had a much easier time borrowing on note or bond inasmuch as his effects were all in the country and not overseas. That this was indeed so can be seen by a quick glance at that least exotic of English trades, the manufacture and export of cloth. In his pioneer work on Leeds, R. G. Wilson found that the raising of additional working capital by bonds (and notes) was commonplace among Leeds merchants. When a small retired dyer died in 1755, his estate of £2,520 included £1,995 in bonds and notes ranging from £10 lent to a hatter to £700 lent to a merchant brother-in-law. Similarly, the small inheritances of the widows, orphans, and spinster sisters of deceased Leeds merchants were frequently invested in loans on bond to active merchants. At a grander level, a rising merchant borrowed £7,000 on bond between 1790 and 1793 from the wealthy Elams (then retiring from trade). About one case, however, Wilson notes: "Joseph Fountaine, Mayor in 1777 and a partner . . . in a leading house 'borrowed' on his own account £5,800 by bond and note between 1782 and 1790 in varying amounts from £50 to £1,200 from 29 different sources. These amounts were *obviously deposits* [italics added] placed with Fountaine since he could easily have obtained far larger loans, being a merchant of great standing in the town, on much more convenient terms."[22] But this is far from "obvious." By deposits we commonly mean sums taken on loan by an eighteenth century businessman, normally without giving bond, in part as a courtesy to the lender, who otherwise would have had difficulty in placing his money. Brewers, we know, accepted deposits to increase their working capital, but merchants in riskier trades had to give bonds to attract equivalent sums. No one, however, not even a brewer, would pay interest and enter into as awkward an obligation as a bond simply to oblige a friend, neighbor, or dependent with surplus cash to invest. Many small bonds rather than one big one might actually be preferred by active businessmen since such bonds were less likely to be called all at once at a difficult time. (Bonds were commonly drawn for six months or a year but were allowed to run for much longer periods; they could, however, be called when overdue.) It is therefore prudent not to dwell on courtesy deposits but to regard all loans on bond or note as normal business transactions on both sides.

Conditions comparable with those described by Wilson can be found elsewhere, including in the Exeter cloth trade, though the documentation there is not so full.[23] William Russell of Birmingham in 1772–1775, at a time when his personal fortune was only about £14,000, was able to borrow from £8,600 to £10,275 on a long-term basis. Most of this was from his brother Thomas and his sisters at 4.5 percent, but £3,000 of it was from a Miss Mary Addyes at 4 percent, presumably a mortgage.[24]

We have even fuller data on borrowing on bond in Glasgow, where the lenders seem to have embraced an even wider circle of the community than that reached by the Tarletons of Liverpool or the Russells of Birmingham. Although after the Seven Years' War there were a few wealthy individuals in Scotland who would lend £1,000 or more to a single firm (Richard Oswald, for example), this was unusual before 1776.[25] The more normal pattern was for lenders to divide their risks by splitting up their limited investment funds into units of £100 or £200, which were then spread among many firms.[26] Bogle, Somervell & Company, a Glasgow firm of about the same size as Nortons of London, had in 1775 a bonded debt of £7,116 spread among twelve creditors (compared with Nortons' £7,500 spread among five); even so, the Bogle, Somervell average bond (£593) was well above the Glasgow norm for the 1760s and 1770s as shown in table 7.[27] This table also shows, however, that the gradual accumulation of wealth in southwest Scotland permitted Glasgow merchants in the 1760s to borrow on bond in average units that were four times the size of those of the 1720s. The marked rise in the size of bonds in the 1730s and 1750s may also reflect the inflow of funds into the bond market in years of low interest rates elsewhere.

Most of the Glasgow lenders lived in or near the town. They included retired merchants and active

Table 7. *The size of bonds securing loans to Glasgow merchants, 1713–1778.*

Period	Number in sample	Average size (in sterling)
1713–1719	7	£68.13.0
1720–1729	71	87.15.0
1730–1739	41	166.13.0
1740–1749	49	159.8.0
1750–1759	74	249.14.0
1760–1769	99	363.9.0
1770–1778	35	365.1.0

Sources: Bonds registered or inventoried in SRA, B10/15 or in SRO, CC9/7/63 and CC9/16/40–81. The sample leaves much to be desired but the trend is clear.

shipmasters, artisans and retailers with more capital than they could use in their own businesses, and trustees of charities, as well as the widows, guardians of minor children, and unmarried daughters of former Glasgow merchants. The occasional laird, clergyman, physician, or university professor who turns up was often related by blood or marriage to the Glasgow merchant world. An ex-colonial governor or an occasional army officer on the Continent or returned from India appears, almost always with local family connections.[28] Quite exceptional were the large sums (up to £3,000 at a time) advanced on bond to Glasgow merchants in the 1770s by the duke of Montrose.[29]

A clearer sense of the investing outlook of the Glasgow petite bourgeoisie can be obtained from the dissection of one document, the premortuary disposition (23 April 1745) of John Robertson, bookbinder and bookseller of Glasgow. Aside from the goods in his shop, the personal estate that he settled upon his daughter and only child (with a life rent of £50 sterling to his wife) consisted of approximately £3,600 sterling invested in forty separate bonds, notes, and accepted bills of exchange representing loans to different firms in Glasgow:

26 bonds	£2,472 sterling	(average £95)
1 note	55 sterling	
13 bills	1,073 sterling	(average £83)

Four of the bills of exchange were from 1743 or earlier and were overdue; the remainder were dated May 1744 or later (usually for six or twelve months) and had not yet expired. Four were for uneven sums and probably represented commercial transactions, particularly two on the Glasgow printer, William Duncan.

The remainder, like the bonds and notes, were for round sums and most likely represented loans. Eight of the bonds were dated 1743 or 1744, twelve came from 1733–1742, and six were dated between 1716 and 1730. Despite their wording, bonds could be very long-term investments. Only two of the bonds were from persons outside Glasgow (a minister and a landed proprietor). Within Glasgow, one was from a lawyer (writer), one from a maltman and a late deacon of the masons, and another from the merchant-proprietors of the "Tannarie and Leather Factorie in Gallowgate of Glasgow"; all the rest were from mere merchants. By thus dividing his estate, Robertson not only sought to assure both income and security but also placed significant resources at the disposal of the mercantile community, including many of the best-known Virginia merchants of the time.[30] A similar investment strategy can be detected in the 1762 inventory of the estate of the retired Glasgow merchant, John Luke of Claythorn; his personal estate of £5,362 included nineteen loans on bond to local merchants, totaling £3,650.[31]

Much the same kind of people, particularly prosperous artisans, shopkeepers, and retired merchants, can be found lending in London between 1720 and 1760, according to the inventories of the London Orphans' Court.[32] However, there is an important difference between the London and Glasgow capital markets. In Glasgow, there appears to have been nothing other than bonds, notes and bills in which lenders could put their money except mortgages, which apparently obtained a slightly lower rate of interest. (At least four-fifths of the Glasgow bonds found in the various Registers of Deeds were for the full legal 5 percent interest throughout the half century 1725–1775, though an occasional 4.5 percent or 4.75 percent rate can be found.)[33] By contrast, the London Orphans' Court inventories show much greater investment in public funds and in the shares, bonds, and annuities of the three great moneyed companies (Bank, East India Company, and South Sea Company). This seems to confirm the suggestion of Peter Dickson that about 90 percent of the British funded debt was held in or near London.[34] Dickson, however, may have misinterpreted one feature of his data. London merchants regularly held company shares and government paper in their own names for the account of investors or speculators overseas, or elsewhere in Great Britain. Hence we ought probably to reduce his 90 percent somewhat.[35] Even so, the London Orphans' inventories reveal heavy holdings of company and government stock, a practice totally lacking in Scotland[36] and quite rare in Liverpool and other English outports.[37] In all probability, the relative scarcity of capital seeking investment in Scotland strengthened the hand of lenders there and left them uninterested in the yields of only 3 or 3.5 percent on public stock prevalent after the refunding operations of Walpole and Henry Pelham, or even the slightly higher rates prevailing during and after the Seven Years' War. Then, too, the volatility in the market prices of government stock may have made such placements highly suspect to investors far from London.

Although Scottish investors showed little interest in the low yields of government stock, Scotland benefited indirectly from the fall of interest rates in England. We cannot yet be sure of all the details, but modern scholarship suggests that interest rates on mortgages followed interest rates on government securities downward with a margin of from 0.5 to 1 percent.[38] When English mortgage rates reached 4 percent or thereabouts, English investors looking for better returns were tempted to send money to Scotland, where higher mortgage rates prevailed.[39] This would have tended to bring down mortgage rates in Scotland too, forcing Scots who sought the full legal 5 percent to leave the mortgage market and look for good bonds. Thus, the rapid growth of the Virginia trade in Glasgow after 1740 may have been facilitated by the influx of English money into the mortgage market, diverting Scottish funds toward the bonds of mercantile houses. We know that when, in the last stages of the Seven Years' War, the yield on depreciated consols reached and exceeded 5 percent and great capital gains were hoped for as a result of the anticipated peace, English and Scottish mortgage holders called in their funds in Scotland and sent them to London for investment in consols. This tended to raise mortgage interest rates in Scotland and encouraged bondholders to switch funds into safer mortgages. The Glasgow merchants who had their bonds called in for payment were thus put under great pressure, which lasted from 1761 through the international crisis of 1763.[40]

Because bonds were recallable, there seems to have been some question in Glasgow as to whether they were an ideal way of raising funds for mercantile working capital. The richest firm, Speirs, Bowman & Company, with fourteen partners, mostly sleeping, had clauses in its contracts of partnership restricting borrowing on bond to only about 25 percent of partners' paid-in capital.[41] By contrast, the partnership contracts of Alexander Cuninghame & Company permitted borrowing on bond up to 100 percent of the value of the stock (or capital) of the firm,[42] while those of Glassford, Gordon, Monteath & Company permitted such borrowing up to 80 percent of capital.[43] Comparable clauses can be found in other partnership agreements, though some firms, both large and small, had no limit.[44] It is no wonder that in the next century these pre-1776 Glasgow firms were remembered as "Joint Stock Companies of Credit," trading on borrowed money.[45]

It is true, of course, that archives tell us more about loans made than about loans refused, more about capital raised than about capital that proved impossible to raise. Only occasionally does correspondence refer to the difficulties or impossibility of raising money at a particular juncture. Nor do contractual documents usually say anything about that eighteenth century underworld where, in a pinch, money could be raised at interest above the legal limit of 5 percent. We know this underworld existed even though we cannot estimate its extent. It was all too easy to lend someone a sum of money on bond, bill, or note and to deduct an extra few percent from the principal before delivering the loan, a deduction that was usually referred to as a premium. Joshua Johnson alludes to such premiums in his letters to his partners but gives no details.[46] However, during the business depression of 1785, another Maryland merchant in London, Uriah Forrest, wrote to a correspondent in America about the difficulty "of obtaining money on Loan here for any Terms. I really believe that no Man here who has Money to dispose of would part with it to the best Men in England under a Premium that would make the Interest equal to 7½ p[er]C[ent] p[er] Ann[um]."[47]

It is even more difficult to suggest totals of bonded debt in the Chesapeake trade than to suggest totals of capital. John King owed £6,286 in bonds and notes at his death in 1734, and he had imported 249,488 pounds of tobacco in the previous year, or about 0.53 percent of British tobacco imports that year. If all tobacco importers were as heavily encumbered with such debt, the total outstanding for all British traders to the Chesapeake should have been something like £1,184,000 at that time, and roughly £2.5 million for the greater trade on the eve of the Revolution. These estimates are most likely too high, because few merchants were in King's branch of the trade or had his credit standing.

In the early 1770s, as already noted, Bogle, Somervell & Company of Glasgow owed £7,116 on bond and John Norton & Son of London owed £7,500. In 1775, the former imported 1890 hogsheads and the latter 798—implying a bonded debt load of £3.15.4 per hogshead for the former and £9.8.0 for the latter. Part of this difference may be ascribable to the different sections of the trade in which these firms were engaged. Norton, like King, dealt in the more expensive York River tobaccos sold in the home market; such tobaccos might have to be kept on hand a relatively long time pending sale and sometimes were sold on credits of up to six months. By contrast, Bogle, Somervell, like other Glasgow houses, dealt primarily in the cheaper tobaccos exported to France, Dunkirk, Holland, and Germany; these were commonly sold more quickly for export, with payment in no more than sixty days, or were equally quickly exported on the account of the owners. Moreover, tobacco sold inland was subject to an import duty after 1759 of over 200 percent secured by an eighteen-month bond, while after 1723 the whole duty was refunded and the bond cancelled when tobacco was reexported. It made good business sense for merchants selling inland to borrow money at 5 percent to pay their customs bonds early and take the 7 percent per annum discount on the bonded duty allowed by the government. Thus, the need for bonded debt should have been substantially higher in the inland than in the reexport trades. If we assume that the 85 percent of imports (circa 100,000 hogsheads in 1771–1775) that were reexported engendered a bonded debt no higher than Bogle, Somervell's while the 15 percent sold domestically required a bonded debt at Norton's level, we get a total bonded debt for Chesapeake houses in Britain in 1771–1775 of about £460,000, a valued assistance to the total capital of £1 million suggested earlier for the trade.[48]

5

Borrowing from Banks

THUS FAR, I have said nothing about credit facilities available through banks. The record here is thin and unclear. Correspondence between British merchants in the Chesapeake trade and their factors and mercantile correspondents in America rarely if ever refers to banks, even in London, the only port where banking facilities were generally available before 1750. The Drawing Office ledgers of the Bank of England suggest that of the several dozen Virginia firms in existence about 1700, only Perry & Lane got help from the Bank, in their case an emergency sixty-day £6,000 advance.[1] But we cannot generalize from this. Since the minutes of the Bank's Committee of the Treasury before 1779 have not survived, we do not know whether bills of exchange drawn from the Chesapeake were regularly accepted for discount, though some undoubtedly were.[2] Joshua Johnson, a merchant in London, informed his partners in Maryland that the Bank would discount the bills he received if he opened a drawing account there. William Lee informed his brother in Virginia that the Bank would discount any American bills with good London (but not Scottish) acceptances. However, neither they nor many other Chesapeake merchants found it worthwhile to open an account at the Bank.[3]

In Glasgow, even before 1750, the banking picture is clearer. There was then only one private bank in the town, that of the Murdochs, active from the 1730s, though the Virginia and West India merchant, James Robertson, had prior to 1740 conducted a "business of exchange" in partnership with his uncle, Robert Robertson, also a merchant of Glasgow.[4] As neither facility was of any great importance, Glasgow down to mid-century had to be dependent on Edinburgh for its banking. In its early decades, the old Bank of Scotland (founded in 1695) offered little service to Glasgow except for an occasional loan on bond to Clydeside merchants in the Virginia trade, including one for £1,000 in 1711 to a group headed by Daniel Campbell of Shawfield.[5] This policy was temporarily modified between November 1725 and February 1726 when eight such loans on bonds (£100–£3,000) were made to Glasgow merchants. (This may have been encouraged by the exceptionally high prices for tobacco in 1725.)[6] Real credit facilities, however, came only with the foundation of the new Royal Bank of Scotland in 1727. Although the original Court of Directors consisted entirely of landowners, judicial officeholders, and handlers of public money(receivers and paymasters), a merchant was soon added in the person of William Alexander of Edinburgh, the agent of the French tobacco monopoly in Scotland. He was the son of a Glasgow merchant and was connected by marriage to the Murdochs, bankers and Virginia mer-

chants of Glasgow.[7] The great historic innovation of
the Royal Bank was the invention of the overdraft on
current account secured by bond. This was a facility
immediately appreciated and utilized by the merchants of Edinburgh. We soon find Glasgow merchants also opening such accounts, usually with a limit
of £400 or £500 but sometimes of £1,000 or £2,000.
The overdrafts available to Glasgow on such accounts
at the Royal Bank in 1751 totaled £15,000 for twenty-
four firms.[8] The old Bank of Scotland had to meet this
competition by offering equivalent services, beginning
in 1729.[9] We soon find most leading Glasgow
Chesapeake merchants with accounts at either one or
the other of the two Edinburgh chartered banks.

Outside London and Edinburgh, about 1750,
there were relatively few banks but a number of protobanking activities about which we know very little. I
have already mentioned the mysterious private bank
of the Murdochs of Glasgow in the 1730s. In Liverpool, the standard accounts tell us, there were no
banks before 1770. However, the accounts of John
Tarleton seem to indicate that he was interested in
some sort of bank there in the 1750s. In his "Compu-
tation of my Fortune the 13. June 1754," Tarleton
shows among his assets a £1,600 share in the stock of
the "new sugar house," also called John Tarleton &
Company. However, in the equivalent account for 26
April 1758, he describes this asset as £2,020.18.11 in
the "Sugar House & Bank" and notes that "this is 350£
more the Profit in the Bank." There is another allusion
to his gains "by the Bank" in the account for 24 March
1759, after which such references disappear. The im-
plication would appear to be that the sugarhouse of

John Tarleton & Company dabbled in some banking functions about 1758–59 but dropped them thereafter.[10]

Rather more detail is given in the accounts for the 1760s and 1770s of John, Samuel & Richard Gurney, merchants of Norwich. The Gurneys kept their financial transactions in an Interest Ledger separate from their Great Ledger. Their financial business consisted essentially of borrowing money at 4 or 4.5 percent and lending some but not all of it out at 5 percent. Many of their debts shown in the Interest Ledger were for round sums, suggesting "deposits" or loans on bond or note (though the precise character of the obligations is not specified). Persons lending to them often appear to have been rentiers rather than traders. In 1768 we find loans to the firm from:

Thomas Harvey Esq.	£10,000
Ann Chuter	6,000
Mary Bowen	2,000
Martha Dyball	2,000
Rebecca Dyball	2,000
Governor of Bethel [Hospital?]	1,000

It is sometimes suggested that wealthy merchants went into banking in the eighteenth century because they had excess funds for which they sought investment outlets. That does not appear to have been the case with the Gurneys, who had quite low cash positions even though their Interest Ledgers showed heavy surpluses of borrowings over loans to others. On 31 December 1767, for example, in their Interest Ledger they owed £64,020 but were owed only £44,176. In a conventional banking business, that would have created a large cash reserve, but they had only £30 cash in Norwich plus £5,481 in the hands of their London correspondents, the manufacturing chemists Timothy Bevan & Son. The explanation would appear to lie in their Great Ledger, where they owed £27,183 but were owed £115,543. Since their capital was only £70,000, they needed the extra £20,000 borrowed via their Interest Ledger to support these great advances to their trading customers.[11] It would thus appear that the prosperity of their mercantile business created liquidity problems that their financial business was designed to rectify. There can be no doubt that liquidity problems were intrinsic to their business, for they sold their Irish yarn to manufacturers on credits of about nine months.[12] Such protobanking might have alleviated liquidity problems of the sponsoring firm, but it hardly provided a general banking service for outside firms.

The years 1750–1775 saw a miniature banking revolution in the ports, foretelling the greater inland banking explosion after 1783 described by Professor L. S. Pressnell.[13] The existing banking structure may have served reasonably well the needs of government and of wealthy landowners who merely needed deposit facilities in London or Edinburgh. It did not do so for the expanding needs of commerce, particularly outside London. The essential feature of the banking revolution in the ports after mid-century was that export merchants and their allies among the big wholesalers (who also had to sell on long credit) took the lead in forming banks that mobilized the wealth of the agricultural sector (particularly through the issue of bank notes) and the savings of lesser traders, prosperous artisans, and professionals in town in order to advance credit to substantial merchants (including the partners in the bank). Through these greater merchants, the benefits of such credit might reach lesser merchants, dealers, and manufacturers, but they were not the primary beneficiaries of the new bank credit. That distinction belonged to the bigger men of the sort who promoted the banks.

The pattern emerged first and most clearly in Glasgow with the foundation of two new banks in 1750, the Ship (Dunlop, Houstoun & Company) and the Glasgow Arms Bank (Cochrane, Murdoch & Company, subsequently Speirs, Murdoch & Company). The first was originally allied to the Bank of Scotland and the second to the Royal Bank, but both soon broke with their Edinburgh patrons and fifteen years of feuding ensued. In 1761, some of the partners of the Glasgow Arms Bank were instrumental in setting up a third bank, the Thistle (Sir Walter Maxwell, James Ritchie & Company). The important thing about these first three Glasgow banks is that almost all their partners were also acting or sleeping partners in mercantile firms trading to the Chesapeake. Conversely, every great Chesapeake house in Glasgow had access to one or more of these three local banks through common partners: Glassford and James Ritchie to both the Arms and Thistle banks, of which they were partners; Speirs to the Arms Bank, in which he and his partners John Bowman and Thomas Hopkirk were interested; Colin Dunlop to the Ship Bank, of which he was managing partner; and William Cuninghame both to the Arms Bank, of which his partners, Andrew Cochrane and John and Peter Murdoch, were managers, and to the Ship, of which a partner in his Maryland firm, Alexander Houstoun, was a manager.[14]

The general pattern observable in Glasgow can

be found repeating itself in Liverpool and Bristol. In Liverpool, whatever Tarleton & Company was doing in the 1750s, the real start of local banking does not seem to have come until after 1770, a full generation later than in Glasgow. One of the first local banks was Arthur Heywood Sons & Company. The Heywoods were active in the slave trade, but not conspicuous in the Chesapeake trade, although Arthur Heywood had served an apprenticeship to John Hardman (active in that trade) and his wife was a granddaughter of John Pemberton, a prominent figure in the slave trade to the Chesapeake earlier in the century. Other banks were to be started later by Henry Clay, Thomas Staniforth, and Joseph Daltera, all long active in Liverpool Chesapeake firms.[15] However, as of 1775, the Chesapeake and West India traders of Liverpool were just beginning to obtain the banking facilities they needed. The situation was a little more advanced in Bristol, which was nearer to the Glasgow than to the Liverpool model. Four banks were established in Bristol between 1750 and 1769, all with close connections to the foreign traders of the port. The links to the Chesapeake trade varied: the Old Bank (1750) included among its partners only one active Virginia merchant, Thomas Knox; the second, Miles's Bank, had two, Michael Miller and Richard Champion; and the fourth, Harford Bank (1769), had at least three, Thomas Deane, Thomas Whitehead, and Edward Harford.[16]

In London, where there had long been a significant number of goldsmith-bankers or bankers in addition to the Bank of England,[17] the technical need for further banking facilities was less obvious than in the provinces. Nevertheless, here too we see signs of a banking revolution after 1750, with the greatest growth coming in two waves: one during the Seven Years' War, raising the number of private banks in London from eighteen in 1754 to thirty-four in 1765; the other just prior to the crash of 1772, raising the number still higher from thirty-four in 1768 to fifty-two in 1774.[18]

The relationship of specific London banks to different sectors of the metropolitan mercantile community in the eighteenth century and the services they rendered to such sectors are far from clear. When, for example, we look at a list of the customers of the London bank of Staples, Baron Dimsdale, Son & Company, we find absolutely no one associated with the Chesapeake tobacco trade, even though this respectable firm (bankers to several directors of the East India Company, the London Assurance, and even the Bank of England) were the London correspondents of the new Merchant Banking Company of Glasgow. However, their customers included Nash, Eddowes & Martin (and Peter Martin, their successor), wholesale linendrapers who supplied great quantities of Irish and other linens to merchants exporting to the Chesapeake and elsewhere in America.[19] A similar absence of Chesapeake connection appears in the 1774 records of Hallifax, Mills, Glyn & Mitton, and of Mason, Currie, James & Yallowley.[20]

We do not see much more of a connection when we look at the first (1766) list for the new London bank of Prescotts, Grote, Culverden & Hollingworth.[21] The principal founders of this bank were George Prescott, an Italian and Russian merchant, and Andrew Grote, a Dutch and German merchant. As Grote, a big buyer of tobacco for export to Holland and Germany, had married a daughter of Joseph Adams, a leading Maryland merchant, and was the brother-in-law of Silvanus Grove, another leading Maryland merchant,[22] one might imagine that he would have been able to attract to his new bank a good number of Maryland and Virginia houses. In actuality, we find only two in the first ledger of the bank, John Buchanan and Robert & James Christie, though Joshua Johnson came later.[23] Grote did, however, recruit the leading Jewish tobacco brokers (Jacob Israel Brandon, and Joshua da Fonseca Brandon) and perhaps through them a number of other Jewish traders, including Moses Israel Fonseca, tobacco merchant, and Israel Levin Salomons, tobacco exporter. He was also able to attract the business of two leading London tobacco manufacturers (Henry Spencer and Thomas Weston) and of the big Rotterdam tobacco dealer, William Davidson. At its start, however, this firm had only a limited association with the Virginia and Maryland trade proper.

Rather closer to the America trade was the Martins bank under its various styles. From the 1720s till the American Revolution, this bank had a small but steady clientele of substantial Chesapeake houses: John Hyde, followed by his sons; James Buchanan, followed by his successors, Hyndman & Lancaster; William Anderson, followed by his son James; and others. These were all quite substantial houses and their long association with Martins suggests a mutually beneficial arrangement.[24]

An even closer association with the Chesapeake trade can be found in the books of the Freame-Barclay bank. This firm appears to have been started in the 1690s by the Quaker Thomas Gould and his son-in-law John Freame. At some unknown time, probably in the 1720s, the partnership ended when John Freame acquired new premises for his own banking business in Lombard Street (the site of the present Barclays headquarters) and Thomas Gould established a separate bank in Cornhill. Gould failed in 1733 but the Freames continued unscathed. From 1736 the business was a partnership of John's son and son-in-law, Joseph Freame and James Barclay, son of David Barclay, the great Cheapside linen merchant. Other families (Smith, Bening, and Bevan) controlled the bank after James Barclay's death in 1766, but the Barclay family interest reemerged as paramount in 1776. Both the founders, Thomas Gould and John Freame, had had side interests in the Virginia trade in the time of Queen Anne, while the Barclay linen house was a great exporter to America, particularly to Pennsylvania, New York, and the West Indies, but also to the Chesapeake.[25]

With its Quaker and American associations, the Freame-Barclay bank attracted a great deal of business from Quaker and other merchants in the Chesapeake trade.[26] Its customers in the 1750s and 1760s included John, Capel, and Osgood Hanbury (the leading Chesapeake merchants of the day), the affiliated house of Tomlinson & Hanbury (government contractors for remitting funds to America during the Seven Years' War), Z. P. Fonnereau (also a government contractor), leading Maryland merchants, including Joseph Adams, Silvanus Grove, Samuel Hyde, Daniel Mildred, and Jonathan Forward (the leading shipper of convicts to Maryland), the Principio Company (Maryland ironworks), Thomas and Richard Penn (the proprietors of Pennsylvania), Gurnell, Hoare & Harman (a prominent Quaker firm that once acted as buying agents for the French tobacco monopoly), Ambrose & John Crowley (great ironware manufacturers and dealers and leading suppliers to the American trade), and understandably, David Barclay & Sons (big linen suppliers to America), and, less understandably for Quakers, Oswald & Company (great Scottish slave traders in London). What is impressive about this list is not so much the numbers as the quality of the American connections. With the exception of Samuel Hyde, who had to give up his business in the 1740s, they were all firms of the greatest solidity. Joshua Johnson later reported that there were only two firms in the Chesapeake trade that always had enough cash to obtain from customs and suppliers the maximum discounts for early payment: those of Osgood Hanbury and Silvanus Grove.[27] This was not idle chatter. The 1755 annual balance for this bank (Freame & Barclay) shows that Hanbury & Company had a balance of £14,618 and Silvanus Grove one of £12,751.

The Freame-Barclay bank was conducted, it would appear, on the most prudent principles. Its otherwise commendable caution and lack of commercial aggressiveness may help explain why it lost its dominant position among the Quaker and American traders. The biggest challenge came from the Hanburys, the great Chesapeake house established in the 1720s by John Hanbury, who married Anne Osgood, daughter of a rich Quaker linendraper. Their son, Osgood Hanbury, was to marry Mary Lloyd, of the Birmingham ironmongery family, establishing the useful Quaker links between export merchants and their principal (linen and ironmongery) suppliers. John

Hanbury was joined in business by his cousin Capel and later by his son Osgood. Their firm (personal "bankers" to the Lords Baltimore) was for several decades the leading Chesapeake firm in London. However, after the death of John Hanbury (1758) and his cousin Capel (1769), Osgood Hanbury began withdrawing his assets from the Chesapeake. The political disturbances of the 1760s and the nonimportation agreements may have had something to do with this decision. His attention, too, was drawn to banking by his brother-in-law, Sampson Lloyd, who founded a bank in Birmingham in 1765. In any event, in 1769–70 Osgood Hanbury put £5,000 of his own money into the establishment of a new London bank, Hanbury, Taylor, Lloyd & Bowman (a London ancestor of Lloyds Bank). The early records of this bank have not survived, but we may reasonably suppose that the Hanbury name attracted many customers from the Chesapeake trading community. When Joshua Johnson arrived in London in 1771 as representative of his Annapolis firm, he immediately opened an account with Hanbury, Taylor, Lloyd & Bowman. However, he found them too unhelpful after the crash of June 1772 and soon transferred his business to Prescotts, Grote & Company. The Freame-Barclay and Hanbury-Lloyd houses also had to compete with other Quaker banks in London, including Bland, Barnett & Hoare (pre-1720) and Mildred & Company (1778).[28]

Very little information has survived about the precise connections of the London Chesapeake merchants with the banking world. What little there is seems to suggest that the very cautious Quaker banks no longer attracted any concentration of the Chesapeake trade business after 1770, despite their own long acquaintance with that milieu. Instead, the merchants then trading to Virginia and Maryland scattered their business around the City: to the aforementioned Quakers (Hanbury, Taylor & Company; Bland, Barnett & Hoare; Smith, Bevan & Bening), but probably more to non-Quakers (Lee, Ayton & Company; Prescotts, Grote & Company; Walpole, Clarke & Bourne; Martins & Company). The list would undoubtedly be longer if the information were fuller.

Although none of the banks about 1770 except Hanburys had close current connections with the Chesapeake trade, others had histories of prior connection.[29] Still others were closely connected to firms that bought tobacco for France,[30] or, like Prescotts, Grote & Company and Barclays, to firms in the German or linen trades, both heavily oriented toward export sales to North America and the West Indies.[31] Credit made available to a firm dealing in British or German linens could, of course, be used to finance export sales as readily as could credit to a firm of export merchants. Then, too, it should be remembered that the German houses of London not only imported linens for reexport to America, but also bought tobacco, rice, coffee, and other American produce for reexport to Germany. This may have influenced Joshua Johnson to switch his banking from Hanbury, Taylor, Lloyd & Bowman to Prescotts, Grote & Company, affiliated as it was with Andrew Grote, Son, & Company, to which he sold substantial quantities of his tobacco.[32]

The connection between banks and mercantile firms in London as in Glasgow was more than genealogical. When the Barclays were reorganizing their family affairs, about 1780, it was specifically provided that the family's linendrapery and mercantile house should continue to receive a special £10,000 "resource" from the family's bank. (An equivalent "resource" was provided by the Lloyds' bank in Birmingham to that family's ironmongery firm.)[33] The surviving accounts of other London banks show that partners were overdrawn to the full amount of their capital investment.[34] It is reasonably clear that many mercantile investors in the new banks of 1750–1775 were—like the Gurneys—not seeking outlets for surplus capital, but rather sources of additional capital useful for their other ventures.

To understand the services that the London and provincial private banks were able to offer the mercantile community, one must keep in mind some of the essential features of those banks. First of all, British nonchartered banks of about 1725–1775 generally had quite modest capitals. Even the very sober Freame-Barclay bank traded on a narrow bottom. In Joseph Freame's time, part of the annual earnings was retained so that the partners' equity gradually rose from £21,310 in 1749 to £32,237 in 1759, after which further growth was minimal. However, following the death of James Barclay and Freame in 1766, the stock was fixed at £20,000 and not allowed to grow till after the end of the century, all profits apparently being distributed.[35] The stock of Martins fluctuated between £12,000 and £18,000 during 1733–1760: it was £15,000 for 1733–1745, then rose temporarily to £18,000, but dropped to £12,375 in 1747–1748 on the withdrawal of Robert Surman, one of the partners; it rose to £15,000 again with the new partnership contract of Christmas 1748 and to £18,000 the next year, but dropped back to £12,000 in 1760.[36] Hanbury, Taylor, Lloyd & Bowman started in 1769–70 with a capital of £20,000.[37] The reputation and business of banks apparently had only a little to do with their book capital. (The partners' other assets were undoubtedly also taken into consideration by their customers.) The new and rather small bank of Mason, Currie, James & Yallowley had a stock of £30,000 in 1774,[38] as did the much larger and more solidly established house of Prescotts, Grote & Company, according to its partnership contract of 1776. Prescotts still had a capital of only £30,000 in the 1790s though their business had considerably expanded by then.[39]

At least one firm, however, followed a policy of plowing back profits and expanding capital. In 1758 the Nottingham mercer and banker, Abel Smith, decided to extend his banking business to London and entered into a partnership with John Payne of London, a linendraper. The new firm of Smith & Payne, with banking offices in both London and Nottingham, had *no* fixed capital by its original partnership contract of 1758, it being agreed that the partners would advance capital as needed. In the event, on John Payne's death in 1764 the stock was £15,000.[40] The firm was then continued with a capital of £16,963.8.7½ under a new contract of 1765, with John Payne's son René taking his place.[41] (By contrast, the stock of the Paynes' linendrapery firm then was £45,000.)[42] By distributing only part of the profits and plowing back the rest, the capital of Smith & Payne (under its various styles) was built up to £49,343 in 1773, to £53,682 in 1778, and to £72,000 by the partnership contract of 1788.[43] Its stock then must have been about the largest of any private bank's in the City.

Outside London there is less information available. Although what became Lloyds Bank was started in Birmingham in 1765 with a capital of only £8,000, the stock of the Bristol Old Bank (Lloyd, Elton & Company) was £27,000 in 1772–1775,[44] a very respectable figure for a provincial house then. In Scotland, the situation was comparable, as is suggested by the capital (or stock) of the Ship Bank (Dunlop, Houstoun & Company) and the larger Glasgow Arms Bank (Cochrane, Murdoch & Company), both creations of the "tobacco lords":

Year	Ship Bank	Glasgow Arms Bank
1750	—	£15,000
1754	£3,750	15,190
1755	4,750	—
1756	5,650	15,750
1757	6,350	22,500
1759	9,150	—
1760	11,100	26,000
1761	12,900	—
1763	15,000	—
1764	12,000	—

After 1763 the impressive growth rate of the capital of the Ship Bank came to an end, and the amount remained about £12,000 from 1764 to 1776.[45] In Edinburgh, it was possible to start a private bank with capitalization no higher than that in Glasgow. In 1775, the mixed banking-merchant firm, Sir William Forbes, James Hunter & Company of Edinburgh, had a stock of £6,211, in addition to the stock of £8,688 of its sister firm, Herries & Company of London, which had the same partners. The next year the two firms split, with Forbes and Hunter keeping the Edinburgh house and giving up their shares in the London firm. They converted the Edinburgh business into a normal bank with a capital of £4,800 in 1783; this had increased to £9,000 by 1788–89 and to £24,000 by 1803. (Herries and his partners had also founded a St. James's Street bank—the future Herries, Farquhar & Company—in the early 1770s with a capital of only £3,600.)

In the 1780s the bank of Sir William Forbes, James Hunter & Company, it would appear, usually had annual profits exceeding or approaching 100 percent of capital:[46]

Year	Capital	Profits
1783	£4,800	£7,400
1788	9,000	7,188
1789	9,000	7,658

Although ratios this high cannot be found elsewhere, banking profits—where information is available—usually appear to have been comfortable. In the depression year of June 1772–June 1773, the Bristol Old Bank distributed all net earnings (£5,382) in interest and profits to its partners, or about 20 percent on its capital of £27,000; in the better year ending June 1775, distributions reached 24 percent.[47] In London, Martins earned and distributed profits of £6,527.10.0 in 1747 and £4,917.12.7 in 1748 on a capital of £12,375, for an average return of 46.24 percent.[48] In 1769, Freame, Smith, Bevan & Bening (the current embodiment of the Freame-Barclay bank) earned and distributed £7,179.16.2, or 35.9 percent on its capital of £20,000.[49] During 1780–1789, Prescotts, Grote & Company, with a contracted capital of £30,000, earned an average of

£8,862 per annum (29.54 percent) and distributed an average of £8,450 (28.17 percent).[50]

It is clear from these earnings figures that prior to the 1790s successful banks had the means at hand to increase their capital much more rapidly than they usually did. That they did not do so suggests that their partners both were cautious about risky expansion and did not consider book capital all that important. Distributed profits invested by the partners in government and other safe stocks and, even better, in conspicuous landed estates were as effectively part of the reserves of the company as the gold in its coffers. Only in the more dangerous atmosphere of the 1790s did a more cautious attitude toward distributing profits appear. Prescotts, Grote & Company, which had distributed almost all its profits in the 1780s, retained about 36.7 percent during 1790–1799.[51]

With such relatively modest capital, the success of the private banks depended in great part on their ability to attract deposits or circulate their bank notes. London private banks gradually ceased issuing bank notes but were quite successful in attracting deposits. London was of course the center of the monetary circulation of the country. Most of the noblemen and more substantial gentlemen visited the capital annually and managed their affairs from there, utilizing City or West End banks. Merchants and wholesale traders throughout the country kept funds (for bill-of-exchange operations) in the hands of their London correspondents; such funds were usually deposited in banks. Government receivers and paymasters also retained substantial balances in London, but were not before 1782 required to keep them in the Bank of England. All these funds were commonly deposited

with London bankers on demand. Thus, the characteristic liabilities of a London private bank (perhaps 90
percent, excluding capital) consisted of demand deposits without interest, withdrawable and transferable by
check. A much smaller proportion of liabilities
(perhaps 10 percent) consisted of funds lent to the
bank on interest (as term or demand deposits) or by
bond or note. The non-interest-bearing demand deposits were usually referred to as the "ledger" debts of
the bank and all others as "notebook" debts. Table 8

Table 8. *Liabilities (excluding stock) of two London banks.*

Year	Ledger debts (demand deposits)	Notebook debts (deposits and loans on interest)
	Martin & Company	
1731	£139,995	£19,477
1734	167,332	25,376
1737	128,994	22,293
1740	274,427	31,492
1743	201,355	23,055
1746	202,890	14,816
1749	193,940	4,937
1752	230,741	6,665
1755	295,168	7,490
1758	198,407	10,890
	Prescotts, Grote & Company	
1781	244,404	4,413
1784	192,350	24,598
1787	261,514	12,609
1790	417,203	14,613
1793	366,763	46,614
1796	289,460	56,243
1799	351,922	50,385

Sources: See note 36 for Martins. For Prescotts, Grote & Company, see
Summary Book (1780–1856) in National Westminster Bank archives.

indicates the sizes of the two kinds of liabilities at two London banks.[52] A similar breakdown for the Freame-Barclay bank is not available, but its level of operations was close to that of Martins. Total liabilities (excluding stock) of Freame & Barclay and its successors fluctuated between £150,000 and £200,000 in the peace years between 1748 and 1756; they rose during the Seven Years' War to a peak of £308,637 in 1757, but reverted to their older, lower levels with the peace. In the 1770s they sometimes slipped into the £130,000–£150,000 range, but moved upwards once more after the firm was reorganized in 1780.[53] There were, of course, smaller firms in the City: for example, Mason, Currie & Company had only £90,136 in such liabilities in 1774.[54]

Outside London, banks had greater difficulty attracting deposits, but they were permitted to issue bank notes. In the provinces, bank notes were frequently a more convenient medium of exchange than the checks favored in the metropolis. Nevertheless, there were real limits to the ability of banks to circulate their notes safely. Abel Smith & Company of Nottingham had only £4,957 in bank notes outstanding at the end of 1780, but £108,545 in deposits.[55] In Bristol, the Old Bank in 1773 had £47,877.15.6 in bank notes outstanding, compared with £46,128.6.5 in interest deposits and about £100,000 in current account deposits. In the more prosperous year 1775, notes outstanding were still only £49,321, but interest deposits had risen to £68,972 and current accounts to about £130,000. Lloyds of Birmingham in 1771 had £33,000 out in notes and £47,000 in deposits.[56]

In poorer Scotland, deposits were much more difficult to obtain, even though banks paid interest on most of such funds. This made bank-note circulation of much greater importance, though its scale ought not to be exaggerated. Rondo Cameron puts the total bank-note circulation of all Scottish banks in 1760 at only £393,000.[57] Thus, the deposits of one or two contemporary London private banks came to more than the total bank-note circulation of Scotland. In Glasgow, the banks associated with the tobacco trade had less success than the Edinburgh banks in attracting deposits and had to push their note circulation aggressively. The Ship and Thistle banks there had circulations of £100,000 and £64,000 respectively in 1763, and the smaller Merchant Banking Company (formed in 1769) had one of £30,000 in 1771.[58] In its early years, the Ship Bank made up for deficiencies in deposits and circulation by borrowing on bond and accepting overdraft facilities (table 9) from its correspondents in Edinburgh (Fairholme & Malcolm; Coutts Brothers & Company) and in London (Andrew Drummond & Company; James Buchanan; Patrick & Robert Macky; Coutts Brothers & Stephen; Yule & Fairholme). Since the bank would have had to pay interest on such overdrafts in addition to the interest paid on bonds and most deposits, its profitability must have been much less than that of a London or even an Edinburgh bank that could attract a fair amount of cash on interest-free deposits. The bank must have felt this, for in 1756–57 the overdraft debt to others disappeared.[59]

An Edinburgh bank that could attract substantial noncommercial funds on current account deposits and on promissory notes (certificates of deposit) at interest was relatively less dependent on its note circulation and had little need for borrowing on bond. Such, at

Table 9. *Liabilities of the Ship Bank of Glasgow, 1752–1757.*

Date	Total liabilities	Bank notes outstanding	Interest deposits	Owed on bond	London overdrafts	Edinburgh overdrafts
7 July 1752	£97,452	£73,368	£2,097	£4,300	£5,749	£2,152
30 Aug. 1753	131,081	76,353	3,530	8,303	5,811	3,582
12 July 1754	76,632	37,795	2,357	10,703	3,609	4,012
10 July 1755	79,990	31,300	3,346	14,800	6,526	2,416
8 July 1756	96,212	43,529	4,081	14,800	16,542	5,937
8 July 1757	97,230	54,679	4,415	20,945	256	0

SOURCE: SRA, TD 161-1, Ship Bank Balance Book. The remaining unspecified liabilities consisted of accepted bills of exchange and demand deposits.

least, is the inference one may draw from the very different accounts of Sir William Forbes, James Hunter & Company in the more prosperous 1780s (table 10).[60]

Not all funds received by private bankers in the ports through deposits, note issue, and other borrowing were available for loans to mercantile or other customers: banks had to keep substantial cash reserves on hand to meet sudden demands. Because London private banks did not then normally discount or rediscount at the Bank of England, they had to maintain cash reserves that were exceptionally high by subsequent standards. The Freame-Barclay bank during 1748–1754 normally maintained a ratio of cash to liabilities (excluding capital) of between 43 and 51 percent. During the Seven Years' War, when its deposits soared, it maintained high liquidity; its cash ratio

Table 10. *Liabilities of Forbes, Hunter & Company, Edinburgh, 1783, 1788, and 1789.*

Type of liability	Dec. 1783	Dec. 1788	Dec. 1789
Bank notes outstanding	£87,000	£93,300	£102,480
Promissory notes at 3 and 4 percent	273,741	351,328	427,774
Promissory notes on demand	0	681	1,108
Bonds, bills, and obligations	0	1,646	2,851
Accounts current	135,678	178,558	237,625
London overdraft	0	23,062	9,937
Stock (capital)	4,800	excluded	9,000
Interest owed	0	11,558	11,954
Total liabilities	501,219	660,134	802,729

Source: NLS, Fettercairn Papers (acc. 4796), box 201.

reached 78.8 percent in the peak year 1756 and was generally between 50 and 67.5 percent throughout the war. From 1768 through the 1770s that ratio was generally allowed to drop to the 25–40 percent level. (We do not know, however, exactly what this bank meant by *cash*, or whether its definition changed over time.)[61]

Martin & Company's ratio of cash (to total liabilities/minus capital) ranged normally from 35 to 60 percent. In the crisis year 1745 or in years when wars were threatened or starting (for example, 1732–1734, 1739–40, 1755–56) Martins maintained cash ratios well over 50 percent, reaching a peak of 77.1 percent in 1755. In less uncertain times, they permitted the ratios to drop as low as 32 percent (1736). In general, Martins appear to have been slightly less cautious than Freame & Barclay during the same years. This is particularly noticeable in their definition of the word *cash*. Although their cash books are singularly uninformative, Martins' annual accounts indicate that their rubric *cash* embraced coin, bank notes, and certain bonds, including those of the East India Company. That is, Martins included as cash certain marketable bonds that did not fluctuate much in price and could be turned into currency quickly.[62]

The downward drift in the Freame-Barclay cash ratios from 1768 on may have reflected a consensus in the City that lower proportions of cash were permissible. This is at least suggested by Prescotts, Grote & Company's balances for 1780–1800. Its cash ratios (to total "deposits") were about 33 percent in the last years of the American War, 1780–1783, but dropped thereafter to about 15–25 percent (1787–1800), rising to 28.9 percent only in the crisis year 1797.[63] The much higher cash ratios prevalent earlier in the century, though, clearly circumscribed the credit potential of the London private banks.

Outside London, the situation was rather different. Since merchants, manufacturers, and landlords all required a regular supply of bills of exchange on London, a large part of the business of provincial and Scottish bankers was buying and selling bills of exchange on London (making their profit in the margin of about 0.5 percent between the rates at which they sold and the rates at which they bought bills). For these and other business reasons (particularly the specie shortage in the provinces), provincial bankers normally kept only part of their reserves at home in cash; the balance was kept on deposit with their London correspondents. In Bristol, for example, the Old Bank's year-end accounts show deposits with its London correspondents (Prescotts, Grote & Company) of £69,498 in 1773 and only £42,117 in cash; in 1775 it was more nearly balanced with £45,459 in London and £43,430 in cash.[64] The fact that both the Ship Bank (Glasgow) and Sir William Forbes, James Hunter & Company (Edinburgh) were overdrawn with their London correspondents does not mean that they did not maintain London balances. The year-end accounts reflect an accounting problem: money was remitted to London in the form of bills of exchange that were credited to the account of the Scottish house only when paid. In 1788, when Forbes, Hunter & Company owed its London, correspondents, Moffatt, Kensingtons & Boler, £23,062, it had £80,148 in London bills in Moffatts' hands awaiting payment—compared with cash holdings in Edinburgh of £76,800 (specie and notes of other banks). In addition, that year

Forbes, Hunter & Company held £30,908 in exchequer bills and £10,477 in East India Company bonds, which (like all similar holdings) were deposited with Moffatts so as to be available for realization when needed. Both at Moffatts and at Martins, such holdings were held in the name of the London agent rather than that of the provincial principal to facilitate immediate sale.[65] London banks (for example, Freames and Martins) also held shares, bonds, and government paper of their own to bolster their liquidity.

Because of the volume and risks of bill traffic, it was difficult for Scottish and provincial banks to get good London correspondents. In order to attract Wickenden, Moffatt & Company, Sir William Forbes had to agree in 1776 to maintain a balance of £5,000 free of interest in London and to pay interest whenever the balance went under that sum. English provincial banks did the same.[66] When the Thistle Bank (Glasgow) was contemplating moving its London agency from Coutts to Smith & Payne, John Glassford for the Thistle also offered to maintain a large enough balance to cover all contingencies; however, since the London banks never allowed interest on these balances, he wanted a waiver of the usual 0.25 percent commission on bill transactions. If Smith & Payne insisted on the commission, he wanted instead permission to overdraw up to £5,000, paying the usual interest. In either case, the Thistle Bank would give Smith & Payne a bond indemnifying it from all loss.[67] Such bonds may have been routinely given by Glaswegians in order to obtain effective London correspondents: in 1763 the Glasgow firm of John Carlile & Company gave a bond for £5,000 to its London correspondent, Malcolm Hamilton & Company, to cover overdrafts and bill operations.[68] Such bonds were the London equivalent of the bonds that Scottish banks required of their customers to cover overdrafts.

After the private banks had set aside up to half or more of their assets in cash, London reserves, company shares and bonds, and government paper, what did they do with the remainder that might have helped the mercantile community? The preferred activity of commercially oriented banks was discounting bills of exchange of not more than sixty (or at most ninety) days' duration. Thus, any Chesapeake or other merchant who banked with a London private bank normally could expect to have some of the bills of exchange he received discounted each year. We should not, however, exaggerate the extent of this facility. In the oldest (1770–1772) ledger of Martin & Company, we find the accounts of two London firms trading to the Chesapeake: Hyndman & Lancaster and William & James Anderson. In August–December 1770, when trade was still slightly sluggish from the aftereffects of the recently expired nonimportation agreements, only 5.7 percent of the credits on Hyndman & Lancaster's account were from bills discounted by Martins. As the trade revived in the boom of 1771 and early 1772, and bills flowed in from America, the percentage of credits arising from such discounts went up to 13.9 percent in 1771 and 19.7 percent in the first half of 1772. (The pattern in the Andersons' account was similar, though slightly more subdued, perhaps because of the death of William Anderson in 1771.) On only one occasion, in October 1771, was there a direct loan (£1,250) by Martins to Hyndman & Lancaster. This, however, only raised the proportion of that firm's credits coming from the bank in 1771 from 13.9 to 15.4 percent.[69] A credit facility of such proportions was obviously a convenience to a merchant firm but hardly a precondition for its operation.

As the direct loan from Martins to Hyndman & Lancaster suggests, most City banks, in addition to discounting bills, did some direct lending usually secured by promissory notes. The Virginia merchant John Norton banked with Cliffe, Walpole & Clarke, bankers having a family connection with the London buying agents of the French tobacco monopoly, Sir Joshua Van Neck and the Honorable Thomas Walpole. Norton's cash book shows that he was able to borrow from these bankers on notes of hand up to £3,000 at a time (and £4,000 in the exceptional circumstances of 1775). These loans were usually for from one to six months, but on one occasion Norton obtained £3,400 for sixteen to eighteen months.[70] Such loans, without adequate security, could cause trouble for banks. When the Scottish bank in London, Neale, James, Fordyce & Down, failed in the crash of June 1772 owing the crown over £33,000 for duties and Scottish land revenues, an inquisition into its assets revealed £16,321 in uncollected personal promissory notes as well as dubious bills and drafts.[71] To avoid such pitfalls, Prescotts, Grote & Company (today a branch of the National Westminster Bank) had a clause in its partnership contract of 1776 restricting loans (on bills or notes) to three months and requiring that notes of hand have at least one endorser as security.[72]

The fuller the surviving records the more diversity we see in bank lending practices. Though the cautious Freame-Barclay bank concentrated heavily on discounting bills of exchange (and a few navy and ordnance bills) for its customers in the America and other trades, on occasion it lent to a few favored customers on the security of notes of hand or even East India Company shares. In addition to relatively numerous modest loans on notes for sixty days or less, its 1769 discount books show longer-term substantial loans on notes to a limited group of customers, including the West India merchant Richard Gosling (£2,000), the Chesapeake merchants Capel & Osgood Hanbury (£2,000), the Principio Company (Maryland iron-works; £600), Thomas Penn (£1200), the linen merchant John Barclay (£450), and the great African merchants, Oswald & Company (£6,000). Some of the notes appear to have been payable on demand but were allowed to run on for a year or more. Such lending on notes had been radically reduced by the early months of 1772 but became more frequent in the months after the crash of June 1772. Then the firm (at that moment styled Smith, Bevan & Bening) lent up to £3,000 at a time for up to sixty days on the security of notes to the kindred houses of Timothy Bevan & Son and David & John Barclay and to a limited number of others.[73] Martins were even more enterprising or risk-inclined. They lent, for example, on the security of company shares, jewels, precious metals, bottomry and other bonds, and government stock, but for them, too, short-term discounting was the predominant form of lending to America and other merchants.[74] (West End as distinct from City banks lent to landowners on mortgages, but that need not concern us here.)[75]

There is little in the London accounts to suggest that overdrafts were of any importance in the City. The year-end totals of debit balances outstanding at

Martins during 1746–1760 were usually only a few hundred pounds, and only reached £2,000 in 1756 and 1760;[76] at Prescotts, Grote & Company in 1780, they totaled £4,200 compared with £204,226 in bills of exchange on hand.[77] In Nottingham, however, overdrafts may have been a normal means of extending credit. The 1780 account of Abel Smith & Company, Nottingham, shows £59,197 due "per ledger," compared with £74,489 in bills of exchange and notes.[78] In Bristol, by contrast, overdrafts were much less important. At the Old Bank some appear in small amounts (under £100), but they were unimportant compared with bills of exchange. Such bills accounted for £102,251 out of £234,386 total assets in 1773 and £168,149 out of £290,460 in 1775. The accounts do not indicate what proportion of these were local bills discounted and what proportion were London bills bought as remittances. The Old Bank's accounts do show, though, that the house sometimes went beyond discounting to help favored customers. In 1773 it was owed over £4,000 by Sedgley, Hilhouse & Randolph, local Virginia merchants. This was perhaps a result of extraordinary help during the crisis of 1772. It was considered a doubtful debt in 1773 and was still unpaid in 1775.[79]

In Scotland, as already noted, overdrafts secured by bonds were the normal mode of bank credit to merchants both at the chartered and at the private banks. The accounts of the Ship Bank of Glasgow in the 1750s show that most such accounts had limits of only £500 or £600 and that £1,500 was the ordinary maximum even if £2,000 was allowed to a few merchant firms in which one of the bank's partners was involved.[80] Such overdraft facilities were obviously a

great convenience to merchants, but their importance
should not be exaggerated any more than should that
of London discount facilities. Of the £7,116 owed on
bond by Bogle, Somervell & Company in 1776, only
£500 was accounted for by the bonded overdraft at the
Glasgow Arms Bank. Since the firm's own capital then
was £16,640, the role of bank credit in its finances was
clearly limited. Equally limited was the role of bank
credit in the affairs of the greater firm of Buchanan,
Simson & Company: of the £32,061 owed by that firm
in 1759, only £2,072 was owed to the Ship Bank, in
which Buchanan was a partner.[81]

One reason why merchants trading abroad could
not get greater credit from banks was that they were
not the best of risks. It is the nature of foreign trade
that merchants all too often have most of their "effects" abroad and thus can offer little physical security
for loans. Advances on warehouse receipts were
known in Holland in the eighteenth century but were
little used at this time by the Chesapeake trade in
Britain. The only valuable warehoused asset a
Chesapeake merchant was likely to have was tobacco,
and this was often reexported quickly. Even while it
was in Britain, tobacco did not make very good security for loans on warehouse receipts since two-thirds
of its value was represented by customs owed to the
crown for which there was usually already a bond
outstanding, and the crown debt would have priority.
Thus the only security a merchant in such a trade
could commonly give was the security of signatures,
whether on bonds or bills of exchange. (A bond usually had at least two signatures, a discounted bill of
exchange three or four.) Although the ability of a firm
to discount thirty- or sixty-day bills of exchange added

usefully to the firm's liquidity, in the long run the larger sums obtained for longer periods by bond were in most cases more important for its overall level of operations.

The only other significant aids a bank offered to a merchant were deposit and checking services. The use of deposit facilities was of long standing: the 1691 inventory of the Virginia merchant William Paggen shows much of his cash in the form of "goldsmiths' notes," something between a modern certificate of deposit and a traveler's check.[82] After the establishment of the Bank of England, they were increasingly replaced by ordinary checks. Even the use of checks, however, was circumscribed by the circulation of bills of exchange. Joshua Johnson's accounts show that in the 1770s accepted bills with less than thirty days to run often circulated in London at par and were heavily used to settle accounts between merchants and other large traders.[83] In Glasgow, Buchanan & Simson's bill book (1760–1762) shows that of bills received (foreign and domestic) far more were passed in circulation to other traders than were discounted at banks.[84]

In summary, by about the 1720s in London and by mid-century in the outports, merchants engaged in foreign trade had become quite aware of their need for banking services: deposit facilities, local transfer by check, inland transfer by bills of exchange, and short-term credit, particularly through discounting bills of exchange. Where banks already existed, as in London and Edinburgh, Chesapeake and other merchants took advantage of the services offered, limited though they may have been. In outports where no such facilities existed, in the years between 1750 and 1775, Virginia and Maryland merchants joined other merchants trading to North America and the West Indies to found banks in Glasgow, Liverpool, and Bristol. The great expansion of private banking in London and the outports in this generation presaged the much greater expansion of inland banking in the decades following 1783. However, no matter how close the merchants were to the new banks, the amount of credit procurable from that source remained extremely limited. Given their limited capital, their difficulties outside London in attracting deposits and circulating their bills, and the extreme prudence then shown everywhere in setting cash ratios and securities for loans, the early banks could meet only a small fraction of the merchants' credit needs.

6

Commercial Credit

I N THE END, all the resources made available to exporting firms by banks, by private individuals on bond or note, and by the partners' own capital subscriptions and loans were not enough in themselves to finance the export of textiles, ironmongery, East India goods, and the like, to the seemingly insatiable markets of North America and the West Indies—insatiable, that is, when credit was available. The Chesapeake market was fully characteristic in its demand for credit but a bit slower than most in payment, for credits advanced there by Glasgow took, on an average, four years to return, at least according to John Glassford.[1] Even with their credit and borrowings, merchants would have been unable to push exports to the tobacco and other American colonies had it not been for that final and crucial resource, normal commercial credit.

Credit was of differing importance in the selling of imported commodities and the buying of export manufactures. On the eve of the American Revolution, about 85 percent of the tobacco imported into

Britain was reexported. This share, as in the case of most other raw materials, was commonly sold for sixty days' credit, and frequently paid for at delivery with a sixty-day bill of exchange or note. When paid for in cash, a discount of 1 percent was normally given for the sixty days, equivalent to 6 percent per annum.[2] The 15 percent of imports sold for domestic consumption appears to have been sold with six to twelve months' credit in Scotland, but for six months or much less in London; when paid earlier than bargained for, some adjustment was made in the price.[3] Since the domestic market took such a small share on the eve of the Revolution, its credit needs were not perceived as a burden. In this respect, conditions were different from those prevailing in the seventeenth century or the first third of the eighteenth century, when the domestic market had taken a much larger fraction of imports and when marketing arrangements for the share exported had been much weaker. In those days it was frequently alleged that importing merchants had either to export on their own account or sell on awkwardly long credits to tobacconists.[4] In the meantime, there had grown up in London (in particular) two classes of buyers with large resources who relieved the Chesapeake merchants there of the need either to export speculatively or to supply long credit at sales: (1) large buyers for export, both the agents of the French monopoly and others who bought for export to Holland, Dunkirk, Bremen, and Hamburg (for example, Hague; Grote; Langkopf, Molling & Rasch; Mee, Son & Cassau; and Coleberg), both on their own account and on order from manufacturers and speculators overseas; and (2) large wholesale tobacconists and tobacco dealers who could buy dozens of hogsheads at a time and who appear to have supplied the lesser manufacturing tobacconists and snuff-makers.[5]

Richard Campbell in the 1740s recognized that great variations in size lay hidden behind the designation "tobacconist" when he advised parents that the capital needed to set up sons in that way might vary from £100 to £5,000—though a mere "snuff man" needed only £50 to £100.[6] In fact, the London probate data seem to indicate three levels of tobacconists. At the lowest level were small men with estates of £50–£500, essentially retailers not normally in touch with importing merchants; they need not concern us.[7] At the next level were true manufacturing tobacconists with estates of about £2,000–£3,000 who clearly bought from importers and who probably could use all the credit they could get.[8] Finally, there was a group of larger tobacco manufacturers with estates over £5,000, some of whom sold semimanufactured products to the smaller manufacturing tobacconists. Members of this group were as rich as or richer than most of the Chesapeake merchants. They included: Sir Richard Levett & Company, with a working capital (net worth) of over £30,000 in 1705; James Sandwell, who left about £6,800 in 1728; Bosworth & Griffith, with a capital of £10,800 in their partnership contract of 1741; Henry Spencer, who left about £9,200 in 1748, and (Job?) Matthews, who is reported to have left £80,000 in 1735.[9]

Outside London, tobacconists appear to have been somewhat smaller and rarely had the resources to buy without credit. In Glasgow, there were also a few firms of dealers or inland merchants that bought tobacco from the importers (often with long credits) for resale in Scotland or England.[10] The importer could give the inland buyer fairly long credit because he himself did not have to pay the approximately 200 percent import duty for eighteen months. Much more important was the lack, outside London, of big native or German merchant houses buying tobacco for reexport. In Glasgow, Whitehaven, and Liverpool, where the tobacco trade was overwhelmingly a reexport trade, only the local agents of the French tobacco monopoly *regularly* bought for export, paying in sixty-day notes. This meant of course that "the French" could drive very hard bargains in glut years for their big cash purchases.[11] When the importing merchants outside London could not or would not sell to the French, they could only export to Rotterdam, Dunkirk, Bremen, or Hamburg at their own risk, or sell to one another, and it could easily be four to six months or more before tobacco shipped to Rotterdam or similar marts could be sold and the proceeds realized. This tied up a lot of capital, which the weaker houses did not have. The necessity of shipping to the Low Countries or Germany on one's own account meant too that the successful houses in Glasgow or Whitehaven needed more working capital for each hogshead imported annually than did equivalent houses in London.

Tobacco, therefore, or at least the 85 percent of it destined for reexport, if it could be sold at all, usually could be sold for cash or on short credit. By contrast, the goods that merchants bought for export to the Chesapeake or elsewhere in the Americas were normally bought on twelve months' credit, particularly in London and Glasgow, where even fifteen or eighteen months' credit was not unknown.[12] (In Liverpool, it was later alleged that goods could be best bought if purchased for one-third cash, one-third at six months' credit, and one-third at twelve months' credit, but there is no evidence that this was normal before the revolutionary war.)[13] Of course, the price charged by the seller included the costs and risks of twelve months' credit. If the exporting merchant could not pay at the end of twelve months, the sellers might give extensions for three, six, or twelve months (as was common after the crash of 1772) and charge interest at 5 percent for the extra time. If the buyer-exporter was in funds and could pay early, the seller gave him a discount at the rate of 10 percent per annum for early payment.[14] A similar discount at the rate of 7 percent per annum was given by the government for early payment of customs on the small portion of imports (15 percent by 1771–1775) retained for home consumption.[15] It was profitable for a merchant, when credit was easy, to borrow money at 5 percent in order to get the 7 percent or 10 percent discount. John Norton, who sold much tobacco for the home market, tried regularly to pay duties early, while Joshua Johnson, whose Maryland tobacco was mostly reexported, tried to use his money to best advantage by getting the 10 percent discount on early payment for goods purchased. Both were forced to give up such advantages in the difficult period following the crisis of 1772.

The consigning planter (accounting for not more than a third of the trade) could get the benefits of these discounts for himself if he maintained a cash balance in the hands of his correspondents in London or Bristol or Liverpool for such purposes. A few very wealthy, prudent planters, such as John Custis, maintained such balances in London and over many decades regularly received the discount on the duty.[16] Few thought it worthwhile to try to get the discount on goods purchased, for no one at a distance could be sure how the price was set between seller and exporting merchant. In Bristol in the last decades before the war, as a competitive attraction, consignment merchants split the discount on the duty fifty-fifty with the planter even though the planter had no funds in their hands.[17] This device suggests that capital was relatively more plentiful in Bristol but by itself was not enough to correct that port's stagnation in the Chesapeake trade.

The goods exported were rarely if ever bought directly from the manufacturers in Britain, but rather from a variety of middlemen. Joshua Johnson tried to go behind the big wholesale suppliers in London and deal directly with manufacturers, but he was able to establish satisfactory relations only with a sailcloth manufacturer at Lichfield. He visited the West Midlands hardware centers but found that the putting-out manufacturers there could not offer extended credit and kept only minimal stocks on hand. As ironware came in from the cottage artificers, Johnson reported, it was forwarded to commission merchants in London and Bristol on whom the putters-out immediately drew; they lacked the resources to deal on credit with exporters. Thus the bigger factors (commission merchants) in London (and to some extent Bristol) financed the iron and many other branches of the putting-out manufactures through at least partial payment (accepting bills of exchange) on receipt of goods.[18] When the factor did *not* have to pay the consignor until he himself was paid (which appears to have been the case with factors in London selling German linens and, to a lesser degree, Irish linens), he could afford to sell to the export merchant on long credit. When, however, the factor was under pressure to pay the consignor relatively quickly—as in the domestic woolen and iron trades—only the richest (for example, the Fludyers in the woolen trade) could afford also to sell to the exporter on long credit. Most factors, being less affluent, sold instead to another level of middleman, the *warehouseman* (including wholesale linendrapers and ironmongers), who in turn supplied both the internal and the export trades on long credit. Thus there appears to have been a distribution of financial function, the factor (through early payment) financing manufacture and the warehouseman (through credit sales) financing distribution.

The role of factors and warehousemen as suppliers of credit in the manufacture and distribution of export goods was the result of a long evolution that can most readily be followed through the example of woolens, which accounted for 47.5 percent of English exports and reexports in 1699–1701. At that time woolens were overwhelmingly (66.1 percent) exported from London.[19] In the first half of the seventeenth century, an inland putting-out manufacturer of woolens could if he wished (and most did) send his woolen cloth up to London and sell it himself or by a servant. As the century wore on, it became far more common to consign such cloth to a Blackwell Hall factor, who sold it on commission. Most initial sales then were for cash or short credit (up to sixty days), but longer credits (about six months), particularly on resales, were not unknown. By law, at least, cloth sent up to London had to go through Blackwell Hall. The abolition of the exclusive privileges of the Merchant Adventurers (in 1689) and the Eastland Company (in 1673), along with the considerable expansion of the export trade to North America and the West Indies during 1660–1700, greatly expanded the number of firms interested in buying woolens for export. These tended to be smaller, weaker firms, which put less emphasis on price than on credit terms. To get their business, factors were forced to concede longer credit terms, so that a twelve-month credit had become commonplace if not universal by the end of the century.[20] There was considerable controversy about this in the 1690s and clothiers tended to fix the blame on the monopolizing tendencies of the Blackwell Hall factors, who by granting long credits prevented smaller men from competing with them.[21] It is not clear that these factors had very much choice. Only those who could give credit could sell. Since clothiers lacked the resources to sustain the whole system of long credit, factors were forced to assume part of the load themselves, particularly by supplying raw wool on credit to clothiers and by letting them draw bills of exchange as soon as they shipped their cloth to London. Factors who could not offer such services would inevitably have lost their clothier correspondents to competitors who could. By the middle of the eighteenth century, Blackwell Hall factors were rather grand figures. Of perhaps the greatest of them it was reported: "Sir Samuel Fludyer, who was factor to most of the great clothiers, used to send them their balance in his own notes instead of money, which circulated in Gloucestershire, and the parts adjacent, for two, three, or four years, without returning to him to be liquidated in bank bills or specie . . .''[22]

Modern understanding of the precise credit and other relations of the Blackwell Hall factor with his suppliers (the clothiers) and with his customers (the drapers and warehousemen) has been rendered all the more difficult by the rarity of surviving factors' papers. In fact, the records of only two eighteenth century Blackwell Hall factors have as yet come to light: a letterbook of Elderton & Hall of the 1760s and letter-books and some other papers of Hanson & Mills of the 1790s.[23] Both firms traded primarily to Gloucester-shire, Wiltshire, and Somersetshire. This was a rela-tively affluent section of the woolen industry, specializing in more expensive cloth made in part from imported Spanish wool. While the poor weavers of the North had to be paid weekly, clothiers in the West Country settled with their weavers as infrequently as twice a year. When one clothier paid a weaver a month early, Elderton & Hall censured him for an unthinking waste of cash and credit.[24]

Elderton & Hall, like Hanson & Mills and other Blackwell Hall factors, normally did not give consign-ing clothiers the names of the firms to whom their cloth had been sold, nor did it inform customers of the names of clothiers whose cloth they had bought. Such secrecy prevented customers (drapers and merchants) from establishing business links with desirable clothiers and thus cutting out the factor.[25] However, in the case of more than one important West Country consignor, Elderton & Hall waived the rule and re-vealed the names of some forty purchasers. This detail establishes that Elderton & Hall's customers were about 90 percent drapers or warehousemen and hardly 10 percent merchants.[26] In its correspondence, Elderton & Hall mentions three types of payment: cash, six-month credit, and twelve-month credit, each with at least a thirty-day grace period. Cash sales were very rare.[27] (The only exception was cloth ordered by Elderton & Hall on its own account: it paid half in cash and half in wool.)[28] Six months' credit was usual on cloth specifically ordered by a customer at a prearranged price.[29] Ordinary commission sales to drapers or merchants could be at six or twelve months' credit, but the latter appears to have been more common.

Theoretically, the clothier was expected to wait until the factor was in cash from a sale before drawing on him. In practice, in order to remain competitive, Elderton & Hall, like other factors, allowed consigning clothiers to draw sixty-day bills upon them immediately for up to half the value of cloths received. (The other half was intended to pay for wool, commissions, transport, and miscellaneous expenses.) (It also sent some of its own notes into the country in payment, in the Fludyer manner.)[30] The house usually set a maximum figure on overdrawing. For its services, it charged the usual 2.5 percent commission on both cloth sales and wool purchases; in addition it charged an optional but conventional extra 2.5 percent to insure or guarantee payment by purchasers (compared with the 0.5 percent usual in trades with shorter durations of credit).[31] Against these substantial commissions, Elderton & Hall frequently waived interest on advances up to a specified limit in order to attract consignments. This was a favor that could be withdrawn if misused, particularly if a clothier used the factor's money to buy wool from another source. Toward the end of the 1760s, Elderton & Hall decided that its system of interest-free advances only made sense for clothiers specializing in superior grades of cloth, from whom the factor earned substantial commissions on purchases of foreign wool and sales of expensive cloth; from the manufacturers of cheap cloth it obtained no commissions on wool purchases, and the little it earned on cloth sales did not cover its expenses and interest. From this latter group it insisted on interest after 1768.[32]

Hanson & Mills's letterbooks are rather less informative than Elderton & Hall's. It also combined selling on commission with ordering cloth at a set price on its own account. Its combined charge for cloth sales and collection insurance could run as high as 6 percent.[33] It sometimes appeared to be waiving commission, but on closer examination such offers usually related to cloth orders and not consignment sales.[34] In the records of both firms, we see the resources of the Blackwell Hall factor fully committed in providing wool on credit and cash advances for his clothier correspondents. There is no reason to think there was anything unusual about the experience of either house.

Thus encumbered, not even the rich Blackwell Hall factors were able to carry the whole load of lengthening export and domestic credits. Even in the long-established European trades, the tendency was for credits to grow from six to twelve months or more as they had in the American trade.[35] The domestic trade was almost as bad.[36] Thus, in the correspondence between London and the colonies, about 1750–1775, we find few references to Blackwell Hall factors as sellers of cloth. Instead, it was to the great draper or warehouseman that the export merchant turned for his supplies. (This may have been legally advisable when the merchant was not a freeman of London.)[37] And just as the factor financed the clothier, so the warehouseman financed the export trade (and much of the inland trade) by selling on credits of twelve months or more.

In the London cloth trade, the situation was further complicated by the activities of packers, who frequently acted as buying brokers. Packers, as their name implies, were originally simply craftsmen who packed woolen goods for export. To this they sometimes added the storage of these valuable goods for merchants who lacked the proper facilities. In London, however, only freemen could buy woolens in Blackwell Hall from clothiers or their factors. Since packers were normally freemen of London and were recognized as possessing expert knowledge about the qualities of woolens, they came in time to be employed as buying agents or brokers for the purchase of woolens by merchants who lacked the skill or were legally unable to execute purchase orders received from abroad. The packer not only selected, purchased, stored, and packed the woolens but arranged for dyeing and helped to a limited degree with credit. Some went behind the backs of the Blackwell Hall factors and ordered cloth directly from manufacturers in the country. In some cases, the exporting merchant did not even know the names of the manufacturers or sellers of the cloth he purchased. Packers normally received no commissions for such additional services but were content with their usual packers' fees.[38]

However, the merchants trading to America, needing the longer credit terms of the warehousemen, tended to avoid the packers, even if others found them useful.

In the half-century preceding the American Revolution, London controls had so weakened that export merchants not free of the city could completely subvert the Blackwell Hall system and order woolens directly from the country, particularly through buying factors in Halifax and elsewhere in Yorkshire, who executed such orders for a modest commission. Although we can find examples of Virginia merchants employing such buying factors,[39] this direct system was not widely used—undoubtedly because it did not offer the credit available from the London warehouseman.

The evolution of the credit and other functions of the factor and warehouseman, relatively clear in the woolen trade, appears also to have taken place in other branches of export-oriented manufacture. The ironware industry of the West Midlands was for the most part also in the hands of small putting-out manufacturers. As already noted, Joshua Johnson in 1771 thought he could go behind the big London ironmongers and buy nails and other ironware more cheaply from manufacturers in Birmingham, Wolverhampton, and other West Midland iron centers. When he visited there, however, he found no substantial dealers with well-assorted stocks, and he learned that the manufacturers could not offer credit but were accustomed to send their goods as they received them to factors in London and Bristol, upon whom they drew bills of exchange immediately. Thus he found it more economical to buy from big ironmongers in London, who would give him twelve months' credit and allow him a discount at the rate of 10 percent per annum for early payment. Lascelles & Maxwell, a big West India firm, had come to the same conclusion in the 1740s. Thus the wholesale ironmonger performed in his trade much the same functions as the warehouseman in the woolen trade.[40]

There were, however, two substantial iron-manufacturing firms outside the Midlands that were affluent enough to deal directly with exporters on long credit. The Crowleys were not only big manufacturers on the Tyne and elsewhere, but they had integrated forward and maintained a large, well-stocked ware-house on the Thames to supply both the home and export markets. Thus a planter in the Cheasapeake could get a barrel of nails from a commission merchant in London with a bill of sale indicating that it had been purchased at the "shop" of "Theodosia Crowley, ironmonger."[41] Much newer was the Scottish Carron Company, founded in 1759, with works near Falkirk between Edinburgh and Glasgow. Its cast-iron ware found an early and substantial market among the Chesapeake and West India merchants of Glasgow. (It also had a warehouse in London.) For many years, the company's own financial plight made it try to limit credit to six months on domestic sales and nine months on Glasgow export sales. However, in the slump following the crash of 1772, it was forced by English competition to extend credit on export sales to twelve months for its Glasgow customers.[42] Taking Great Britain as a whole, however, the forward inte-gration of the Crowleys and the Carron Company was exceptional. The lesser iron manufacturers of England had a great need throughout the century for the ser-vices of factors and wholesale ironmongers.

There were also factors in London who received linens on consignment (for sale on commission) from Germany, Ireland, and Scotland. Though the linen trade in England still awaits its historian, certain rather tentative points can be made. The situation of the linen factors in London was rather different from that of factors receiving English woolens and ironmongery. Non-English linens were, it would appear, usually consigned not by small manufacturers but by fairly substantial merchants in Bremen, Hamburg, Dublin, Edinburgh, and elsewhere, and later by big printers in the north of Ireland, none of whom appears to have been dependent on the London factors for credit advances and all of whom appear to have been able to wait a little while for payment—whether they liked it or not. The factors receiving linens from Germany appear to have been particularly strong and could sell to export merchants on the same long terms as wholesale linendrapers. The factors receiving linens from Ireland were less able to compete because they were kept on tighter rein by their principals in Ireland. In the 1730s we hear of Dublin linen merchants resisting the factors' arguments for extending credit on London sales from six to nine months.[43] In the 1770s Joshua Johnson found that he could get only six months' credit from an Irish factor (such as David Harvey) but could get twelve months' credit from wholesale linendrapers (such as Barclays, or Nash, Eddowes & Martin). Then too the factors handling German and Irish linens in London normally sold such textiles only in the package (bale) as received from the overseas consignor. This was not always convenient for the export merchant (or inland trader, for that matter), who found it more convenient to go to the big wholesale linendrapers, such as Barclays, who were not factors and, trading on their own, could break open bales and supply quantities and assortments as desired. Just as some of the big woolen warehousemen went behind the factors and ordered directly from country manufacturers, so Barclays maintained buying agents in Ireland who purchased directly at the fairs and from the manufacturers or printers and thus eliminated the middleman in both the Irish ports and London. Some London linendrapers also ordered directly from Germany. Such firms had the resources to combine the credit functions of factor and warehouseman. (In fact, Barclays and others were sometimes their own export merchants.)[44]

The factors handling Scottish linen consignments in London in the half-century or so after the Union (1707) appear to have been persons of limited means who let their principals in Scotland draw for reimbursement only after they had collected from those to whom they had sold their linens. This involved long waits that were irksome both to the smaller Scottish linen merchants and to the newer British Linen Company, chartered in 1746 with an initial capital of £50,000 (later £70,000). After mid-century, some London factors allowed Scottish consignors to draw on them twelve months after shipment whether or not payment had been received from sale. By the 1760s, competition induced some substantial factors to permit Scottish correspondents to draw on them immediately on shipment for up to half the value of linen consigned.[45] This is about as much credit as Blackwell Hall factors normally offered their consignors and suggests that by the 1760s some London factors handling Scottish linen were rich enough to support the capital-intensive Blackwell Hall style of business. The Scots factors, too, normally sold not directly to export merchants but to big wholesalers who in turn supplied the export merchants with wider selections and longer credits.

The big warehousemen, linendrapers, and iron-mongers are an almost unstudied group.[46] Yet without them we cannot understand the financing of the export or even the inland trade. Defoe in 1730 saw the lines of trade and credit that tied the whole country to-gether. Petty shopkeepers all over the country, he pointed out, were supplied on credit by larger dealers in their several lines in the principal towns; these dealers in turn were supplied on credit by the met-ropolitan "Wholesale Men." "These Wholesale Men in *London* are indeed the support of the whole Trade, they give Credit to the Country Tradesmen and even to the [export] Merchants themselves; so that both Home Trade and Foreign Trade is in a great measure carried upon their Stocks."[47]

How great were these "stocks" that enabled warehousemen and other metropolitan wholesalers to support so much of the trade of the country? Really substantial wholesalers in London must have had capi-tal equal to that of the average exporter, and the greater of them must have towered over most of the merchants with whom they dealt.

Davison, Newman & Company, for example, were wholesale "Grocers Tea Dealers and Confection-ers" of Fenchurch Street, London, conducting a well-established business going back to the middle of the seventeenth century. Most of the company's trade was inland, but it sold grocery and teas to merchants trading to the West Indies and North America, including (about 1754–1757) the Chesapeake traders John Buchanan, James Buchanan, Anthony Bacon, James Russell, Matthias Gale, William Anderson, and Sydenham & Hodgson, as well as William Miller of Bristol and Glassfords of Glasgow (through the latter's London correspondents, Claude Johnson & Son). Although grocery was normally a short-credit business, the account of James Russell shows that credits of six months and longer were arranged. The capital employed in Davison, Newman's business in 1781 was £122,000: £80,000 original (1776 partnership) capital, £24,000 accumulated profits left in the business, and £18,000 borrowed.[48] It is doubtful if a single North America merchant in London (except Hanburys and maybe one or two others) had a capital equal to that of these grocers.

It would be extremely helpful if we had accounts similar to those of Davison, Newman for other branches of London trade in which big wholesalers were active. We know that John Crowley, the great ironmonger, left a personal estate of over £140,000 in 1728, but he was a manufacturer as well as a wholesale ironmonger and it is difficult to establish what proportion of his capital should be ascribed to manufacturing.[49] In any event, everything about the Crowleys' affairs was exceptionally large. In the textile trades we are not much better off. Thomas Cullum started as a wholesale woolendraper in 1624 with a capital of £2,119 and had increased his stock to £29,102 by 1641. We know about some other early seventeenth century cloth dealers with capital in the £12,000–£32,000 range, but they appear to have been exporters as well as wholesalers.[50] By the mid-eighteenth century, capitalizations in all fields were generally much larger. In London, even a stationer-printer might have a capital of £50,000,[51] and West End lacemen and mercers with entirely retail trades had capitalizations of £4,000–£12,000.[52] The few City wholesale mercers, linendrapers, silk dealers, haberdashers, and hatters of whom we have record generally had capitalizations then in the £4,000–£20,000 range (quite respectable by the standards of contemporary Chesapeake merchants).[53]

Nevertheless, some relatively small people ventured into the wholesale trades supplying exporters, particularly before 1750. William Cary, a citizen and haberdasher of London, left a personal estate of only about £2,500 when he died in 1664–65. The basis of his trade was native and imported wools, Barbados and Smyrna cotton, Lancashire cotton yarn, and German, Scottish, and English linen yarns, which he supplied to manufacturers in Lancashire and elsewhere. In return he received linen, cotton, and other fabrics, which he sold to exporters and exported on his own account, particularly to his Cary relations in Virginia. They sent him Virginia tobacco in return.[54] It was all very diffused and small-scale in comparison with the next century, when greater specialization and greater volume were generally the rule. Still, somewhat comparable was the business of Jacob Wyan, citizen and draper of London, a small whoesale mercer who died in 1730 leaving an estate of under £5,000. His stock in trade consisted primarily of silks and mixed fabrics with some woolens. He sold these to well-known export merchants, including such traders to the Chesapeake as Brian Philpot, Benjamin Bradley, and Jonathan Scarth. He also exported directly to the West Indies and North America, including Pennsylvania. In return, some of his West Indies and Chesapeake correspondents sent him small consignments of sugar and tobacco, some of which he sold through a Mr. Coward. He had taken a $\frac{1}{32}$ share in a ship managed by John Falconar, a Maryland merchant of London, and had stood surety on the tobacco bonds of John Midford, a Virginia merchant of London who had failed. He was obviously overextended for a person of his relatively modest means.[55] More typical perhaps of the smaller men was William Markes, a Cheapside glover, who left an estate of about £4,000 in 1736 and included among his customers such respectable export traders as John Hanbury and David Barclay & Son.[56] On a similar scale was Richard Kennet, a glass-seller of New Fish Street (Fish Street Hill), London, who left an estate of £4,460 in 1735. His customers included leading Chesapeake merchants such as John Philpot, James Buchanan, Neil Buchanan, Philip Smith, and Jonathan Forward.[57]

However, in the half-century preceding the American Revolution, there gradually emerged in London and the greater outports a number of much larger wholesale linendrapers and the like, part of whose business lay in supplying the export trade. The London linendrapers Payne & Swayne had a capital of £12,000 in 1728, rising to £20,000 in 1731, £26,000 in 1734, £30,000 in 1738, and £42,000 in 1742. After the withdrawal of partners John Payne the elder and Thomas Swayne, the firm was continued by Payne's two sons, John (the younger) and Edward, with a capital of £40,000 in 1751 rising to £48,000 in 1757 and about £80,000 in 1764. (The brothers were quite eminent for "linendrapers": John, a director and governor of the East India Company, joined Abel Smith in

1758 to found the London bank of Smith & Payne, while Edward became a director and later governor of the Bank of England.) John Payne withdrew (and died) in 1764, taking a good bit of capital out of the firm, but the house was continued by Edward and John's son René Payne with an initial capital of £45,000.[58]

There were undoubtedly a fair number of other textile wholesalers in London who, if less distinguished, still had capital comparable with that of the Paynes. Particularly conspicuous in the America trades were the major firms of Barclays in linens and Mauduit, Wright & Company in woolens. When the Chesapeake merchants Perkins, Buchanan & Brown went under in the depression of 1772–1773, they transferred to their linen suppliers, Barlow, Wigginton & Francis, £30,000 worth of debts owed them in America! The partners of the latter firm (Andrew Barlow, John Wigginton, William Francis) had also been signing Perkins, Buchanan & Brown's customs bonds for them.[59]

In Bristol, Fisher, Baker & Griffin, wholesale linendrapers, had a capital of £18,000 in 1739, £30,000 in 1747, and £36,000 in 1754. This firm too was very close to the export trade, with Paul Fisher, the principal partner ($\frac{7}{12}$), signing the customs bonds of John King, Virginia merchant.[60] Liverpool may not have had an equivalent need for big linendrapers, for it had access to the big wholesale linen and cotton dealers of Manchester. In addition, it had by the 1750s attracted at least one German firm, Fuhrer & Wagner, selling (on commission) linens received from Bremen to Liverpool's export trade.[61]

In Glasgow, there was a shortage of such big

warehousemen, to the evident embarrassment of the Chesapeake trade. An ordinary merchant about 1760 might have had to deal with a dozen linendrapers or small warehousemen simply to buy the several varieties of linen he needed for a single shipment to a single store.[62] To get around this, we find a group of big "tobacco lords" (including Provosts Andrew Cochrane and John and George Murdoch) acting together in 1759 to set up a big "universal warehouse" with a capital of £12,000, the largest known firm of its kind then in Glasgow.[63] The bigger firms tried their own integration. Ingram & Glassford, starting out as warehousemen, integrated backward into linen manufacture and forward into exporting. Colin Dunlop persuaded James Wilson & Sons, merchants and linen manufacturers at Kilmarnock, to take a quarter or half share in three of his Chesapeake companies. Two other Chesapeake merchants, James McCall and Robert Scott, entered into a linen manufacturing and trading partnership in 1765 with the brothers Edward and James Finlay, the latter of whom was later to become a pioneer cotton spinner.[64] And other examples could be given.

In summary, the warehouseman-wholesaler selling to exporters and the use of long credit became the most striking characteristics of British foreign trade in the eighteenth century. The solidity of both the warehouseman and the export merchant compensated for the risks of credit. Some manufacturers and warehousemen refused to accept orders from abroad, insisting on selling, though on generous credit terms, only to firms domiciled in Great Britain. In 1784, John Carter, a merchant at Williamsburg, Virginia, tried to establish a direct link with the long-established firm of

Davies, Jones & Company, which manufactured hats at Stockport, Cheshire, and had offices in London and Bristol (and an agency in Glasgow). The company replied, "We shall be very happy to serve You with hats in which branch we do very Considerably in the Export way to the West Indies and now to All parts of North America but we must beg leave to Acquaint you that we continue to adhere to the late Mr. Rosseter's Plan which is never to send out any goods on our own Account, but allways have a House here to Apply to for payment when the money becomes due, which Credit is twelve months; If You will please to Appoint any House of Credit here to be our pay Master, we will most Chearfully execute Your Order . . ." Much the same answer went to a like inquiry from Bayonne. In a similar vein, the wholesale pewterer, Richard King, refused to accept a direct order from Samuel McCall of Philadelphia.[65]

This warehouseman–long credit export system was recognized as a peculiarity of British commercial organization that was not characteristic of Continental countries. It probably had its origins in the institutions of rural credit prevalent in England long before the great post-1660 expansion of the colonial export trades.[66] Some saw this credit as an English answer to the problems of capital shortage and relatively high interest rates. In a well-known passage of the 1660s Sir Josiah Child argued that the English trader could not compete with the Dutch in neutral markets because the Englishman had to pay 6 percent for his capital and the Dutchman only 3 percent.[67] In effect the Englishman's answer was a generalized system of easy credit. Charles Carlton's data on fifty-seven estates reported to the London Orphans' Court in

1662–63 show that for every £100 in personal physical assets (including leaseholds but not freeholds) there were £46.8.0 owed by and £103.10.0 owing to the estate.[68] What is not usually realized is that little changed in the ensuing century; if anything, the situation became more acute. In 1784 John Hope, the British-Dutch banker, published his *Letters on Credit*, written just after the crash of 1772. He saw the problems right after the crash in monetary terms, a shortage of currency that was causing both high interest rates and long credits:

> In Holland and Flanders, where money is plenty, the interest of it, as it was but lately, is often as low as three and an half *per cent.* and the longest credit, given for goods bought in Holland is but six weeks, at which time they must be paid for as punctually as a bill of exchange. The case is very different with us; no merchant can borrow money under five *per cent.* and no American or West Indian merchant can fulfill all the orders of his correspondence, without asking credit of his tradesmen [suppliers] till there is time to expect his returns. Hence proceeds the long credit given for goods, from nine months to two years.

Hope saw the British undone by their own good nature: "They are of all nations the least difficult to treat with, and the most averse, through motives of personal interest, from distressing their neighbours; and thence partly their unbounded trust to one another."[69] In the long run, of course, it was this availability of credit that attracted American business back to British ports after independence—as well as the business of many other unattached nations.

In the short run, however, such easy credit could create fearful liquidity problems for manufacturers, warehousemen, and merchants whenever the normal course of business was interrupted. To avoid this, individual businessmen sometimes attempted to work out quasi-barter arrangements, which speeded up payments and probably increased the volume of transactions that could be sustained by a given money supply. At the beginning of the century the London merchants Benjamin and James Braine appear to have specialized in both tobacco and linen, not just in the Chesapeake but in England and Europe as well.[70] These were commodities that could be readily exchanged for each other in many ports between the Chesapeake and the Baltic. The Braines could not have been too successful, for few attempted to imitate their precise combination—yet many moved in the same direction. In London, as the century progressed, there developed on a limited scale certain informal arrangements to ease the payments problem of the long credits for export. Suppliers of export goods to the Chesapeake trade might also become buyers of tobacco and iron to facilitate the collection of debts and speed up the turnover of their capital. The Crowleys sold hardware to Virginia and Maryland merchants and bought from them the pig iron received as ballast in tobacco ships from the Chesapeake. This balancing act was, however, more common in the case of textiles and tobacco.[71] Thus, by the 1760s the long-established Southwark firm of wholesale haberdashers selling for export, Lardner & Baratty, appears on accounts of sale as a buyer of tobacco. From 1763 on, this dual nature of its business was recognized by its description in the London directories as "haberdashers and tobacconists." The unwary might conjure up a picture of a small shopkeeper branching out. In fact, the firm's dealings in both lines were wholesale. And this case was not unique.[72] William Willy & Company, linendrapers, also bought tobacco. At an even higher level, the prominent London firm of Furstenau, Schroeder & Company, later Langkopf, Molling & Rasch, appears in the records of Virginia and Maryland firms of London both as a big buyer of tobacco and as a supplier of German linens. A comparable role was played by other London firms dealing in the same way: Sutton & Schombart; the Dutch and Hamburg merchants, Mee, Son & Cassau; and the Bremen firm in London, Kruger & Grote, later Andrew Grote & Son.[73]

In summary, in a commercial world with a money supply perceived as inadequate and a primitive banking system, commercial credit performed at least three valuable functions. First, insofar as a great range of commercial transactions could be handled simply by debit or credit entries in open accounts, the use of scarce money (hard or paper) could be dispensed with, at least in the short run. Second, insofar as early-dated and relatively small bills of exchange and Blackwell Hall factors' notes passed readily from hand to hand, the effective money supply was increased. Finally, credit brought into use resources that otherwise might have remained idle. A West Country weaver accepted delayed payment for his labor when the alternative might be unemployment. A clothier agreed to have his cloth sold on credit when the alternative might be to let his labor force and capital lie idle. The factor, draper, ironmonger, and warehouseman sold their goods on long credits (and at appropriate prices) because otherwise there was a good chance that those goods would sit unsold on their shelves, and they counted the risk of nonpayment (already provided for in the price) as less costly than the certain loss of income from their capital if the goods were not sold until a cash customer appeared. The export merchant trading on his own account was persuaded to sell his wares to colonial traders and planters on long credit because he could cover risks and delays in the price and expected through such favors to obtain surer return cargoes of tobacco or other colonial produce; he must have calculated that this was the most productive way to use his limited capital. The British credit system thus would appear to have resulted in a greater total production of goods and services and in a higher return on risk capital, at the cost, perhaps, of a higher failure rate and possibly higher retail prices. It is true that in theory the cost of credit should have raised retail prices and thus restricted demand, but the availability of retail credit may simultaneously have enhanced consumer demand. However, the availability of credit to manufacturers and merchants should have increased supply and probably moderated prices. It is unlikely, therefore, that the combined effect would have been a rise in retail price and a restriction of consumption.[74]

How much commercial credit may have been involved in the aggregate in the American trades? I can only offer the most tentative estimates. As explained in chapter 2, Richard Champion estimated that a total of £6 million was owed by the American colonies to Britain in 1774 before the repayments of 1775. (This figure presumably included both debts and unsold goods in America.) If prewar debt was distributed in the same proportions as postwar debt claims, then about two-thirds of it, or £4 million, would have been owing from the tobacco colonies of Virginia, Maryland, and North Carolina. From this about 20 percent should be deducted for profit margins, leaving a net British stake in these debts of about £3.2 million.[75] To this about £800,000 should be added for British investment both in ships trading to these colonies and in colonial real estate (stores, warehouses), making a total venture of about £4 million. I have previously suggested that the firm capital involved in the tobacco trade was in the vicinity of £1 million and that at a conservative estimate something like £460,000 was borrowed on bond. If we assume that another £100,000 was provided by banks and up to £440,000 by outside investors in the trade's ships and real estate, then £2 million is still left to be accounted for by commercial credit. For the entire North American-West Indian-West African trading complex in 1774, the figure may have been as high as £9 million. These calculations are anything but certain, but they do suggest that commercial credit made a far from minor contribution to the financing of British overseas trade before the American Revolution.

7

The Significance of Credit in the Chesapeake and the Financial Crisis of 1772

WHAT did this system of capital mobilization and credit mean for the planters of Virginia and Maryland? The presence of a cash market for tobacco (particularly in London) and of easy sales to the agents of the French monopoly in Glasgow and the other north-western ports, combined with the long credits available to exporters buying textiles, iron-mongery, and other British manufactures, meant that it took a comparatively modest capital amount to set up in the Chesapeake trade, particularly as a consignment merchant. This kept the number of exporting firms in the trade relatively large (over 150 in 1775), though not all firms that exported goods imported tobacco. That this much competition did not lead to a shrinking of the substantial markups (or advances) that British manufactures underwent before reaching the planter was no doubt due to the real costs involved in the long credits offered by the export merchant in Britain, which rested in turn upon the long credits available from the wholesaler.[1] There is, as we are told, no such thing as a free lunch.

The credit that warehousemen and other whole-salers allowed to export merchants reached the Chesapeake in different forms at different levels. The tenant farmer or the newly established small independent proprietor with no slaves and relatively unimproved land had little or no "estate" to guarantee advances but could usually obtain some credit from a local shopkeeper or from the nearby "store" of a Glasgow, Whitehaven, or Liverpool firm. Archibald Henderson, a prominent Glasgow merchant, explained in 1766 the ability of the propertyless to obtain credit from Glasgow stores:

> The trade of Glasgow with these two Colonies is of a retail kind. Agents, or Factors, receaving annual stipends, are established by our Merchants in these Governments. These Agents sell to the inhabitants such kinds of European and East Indian goods as are sent them from Britain by their Employers. In payment of the goods they so dispose of, they received tobacco, which, they ship to Glasgow for account of their owners in ships sent out to them to be loaded. The Agents, in disposing of the goods that are consigned them, do not always depend for payment on the real ability of the people to whom they sell them, but often trust to the labor and industry of many, who are in the Possession of little or no real property . . . In a young country where land may be got at a low rent, and where a valuable staple is raised, young men soon leave their Parents, and marrying, settle plantations for themselves. But, in order to make this settlement, they must have some household furniture and working tools. With these, they are supplied upon Credit, by some Factor or Store keeper as he is called. And, thus it appears, that it is in dependence on the labor industry and honesty of many, not of their real property, that they get goods upon credit from different store keepers.

. . . You will easily conceive . . . not only how diffusive the credit has been, but also how small the sums due from many of the debtors must be. And, when you further consider the rivalships in business from a number of traders on the one hand, and that turn for dissipation so natural to a people not enough controlled in the intent of credit given them on the other hand, you will easily account for many of the inhabitants of Virginia and Maryland being at this time so much in debt as they really are.[2]

Such small credits to the small men of the Chesapeake interior were characteristic of the business of the Glasgow houses, particularly the Cuninghame firms. Since these small men could easily throw up their tenancies and move on, such credit demanded the constant attention of the storekeeper, colonial native or Scots. In the long interruption caused by the American War, many of these small men died or moved away, and it was the Cuninghame case in particular that caused the greatest trouble for the international commissioners who looked into the debt problem in the late 1790s.[3]

Quite distinct from these small "dirt farmers" were the substantial planters who owned mortgageable improved lands and slaves. They could deal directly with a commission merchant in Britain or with local native or Scottish stores. Some of them, as John Wayles insisted, were profligate and went in for conspicuous consumption, "Turkey carpets" and all, but as a class they had a keen sense of economic reality and their own best interest. They knew that land values were constantly improving and that one should at all costs, whenever possible, avoid mortgaging land and slaves—except to buy more land and slaves. As legislators, they tried to protect such property from seizure for ordinary debts,[4] and as county court judges they knew how to use the law's delays to protect their kind.[5] However, unlike the small farmers, they were rich enough to be sued and could, if pressed hard enough, be forced to give bonds or even mortgages to hold off a creditor. (Since local creditors were more numerous than British, the pressure to enforce laws on debt was heavy.)[6]

At a still higher level on the scale of business transactions were the native merchants of the Chesapeake. Lacking the capital to compete with the richer merchants of London and Glasgow, they had historically concentrated their efforts, insofar as they traded abroad at all, first on the West Indies trade and then on the wheat and flour trade to southern Europe. From these trades they earned credits in London that they could use to buy goods from Britain or from the local representatives of British firms. When their reputation was sufficiently established, they could obtain shipments of goods from London (in particular) under a credit arrangement known as the "cargo trade." On the receipt of an order from a trusted Chesapeake trader, a London commission merchant would purchase for him a cargo of goods (sometimes worth up to £5,000 or more by the early 1770s) from various London warehousemen, on the usual twelve months' credit terms. It was understood that the Chesapeake merchant would remit tobacco or bills of exchange to pay for the goods in twelve months. The London commission merchant who assumed the burden of the debts for these sometimes great cargoes profited from the commissions on the purchase of the goods and on the sale of any tobacco returned in payment, as well as from the general assistance that the Chesapeake merchant could provide in procuring consignments and other business for him in America and in speeding the return of his ships.[7] Cargo-trade shipments were also made on a limited scale from Glasgow to independent Scottish merchants established in Virginia.[8]

The most dynamic feature of the Chesapeake economy in the years 1763–1774 appears to have been the growth of the independent indigenous merchant and of the cargo system. There had of course been merchants in the Chesapeake since the early seventeenth century, but for those who were not simply peddlers or country shopkeepers, ventures by sea tended to be toward the West Indies, where their limited capital could be more fruitfully employed. Although traces of the cargo system can be found as early as the 1720s,[9] it appears to have been of only marginal importance until the 1760s. Then, three conditions led to its substantial expansion: (1) higher prices for cereals in Europe, which converted many small shippers of flour and victuals to the West Indies into big shippers of grain and flour to Spain, Portugal, and the Mediterranean (and in years of exceptional shortage to France, Britain, and Ireland) in touch with the biggest speculators in London, and which gave the whole Chesapeake additional remittances to Europe; (2) higher prices for tobacco in the late 1760s, which put many planters in funds and made some of them keen to branch out more widely into trade; and (3) easier credit in Britain in the years prior to the panic of 1772, which encouraged many merchants in London in particular to push their trade beyond the limits of the stagnant consignment system, that is, to attract consignments by sending out cargoes rather than waiting passively for business. In addition, the removal of most of the Townshend duties in 1770 led to the collapse of the nonimportation agreements and a rash of orders from America and speculative exports from Britain, all helping to create a mood of commercial optimism and expansion during 1770–1772.

At the height of the excitement in 1770, Thomas Adams, a Richmond merchant, wrote to Perkins, Buchanan & Brown, a newly expanded London house oriented toward the cargo trade:

> The Virginians seem to be gaining ground fast on the Glasgow Men in the Tob[acc]o Trade . . . the Principal Planters from the great Prices they have lately got for their Commodities are entirely out of Debt & choose to be their own Bankers or to leave their Money in the Hands of Men of more Permanent Property [that is, merchants who owned land in the Chesapeake]; this prospect of Things has induced many Gentlemen to enter into Trade & you may depend no Considerable Consignment can in future be received at your Port but by sending Cargoes of Goods . . . I mention it as more eligible to send four or five thousand Pounds annually to Men, who purchase & remit to the Amount of five or six hundred hogsheads Tob[acc]o per Year, then to be half the Money in Advance for a Gentleman [planter] who makes fifty or sixty hogsheads . . .[10]

A conservative firm like John Norton & Sons, which handled requests for cargoes with great restraint, nevertheless saw their outstanding American debts rise from £11,000 in 1769 to £40,000 in 1773, a rather impressive total for a firm with £6,000 capital.[11] Greater speculators in the cargo trade, such as James Russell, William Molleson, and Christopher Court, were reported to have had sums in the vicinity of

£100,000 owing them in America.[12] This suggests that a dozen or fewer correspondents in the cargo trade as it was conducted about 1772 could run up debts equal to those of hundreds of small customers at the Glasgow stores.

These were the institutional arrangements prevailing on the eve of the crisis of 1772. The crisis is usually ascribed to excessive speculation in East India Company shares and in bill-of-exchange operations between London and Scotland. It also had American roots. The nonimportation agreements provoked by the Townshend duties of 1767 broke down after most of the duties were removed in 1770. As already noted, this helped to stimulate a great flood of shipments of British goods to America in 1771 (the peak year for such shipments until the 1790s). Shortage was soon succeeded by glut. In the Chesapeake, difficulties were complicated by developments in the tobacco trade. Relatively poor crops in the later 1760s had resulted in very good prices for tobacco. However, record crops in the five years starting in 1770 were to lead to record importations into Great Britain between 1771 and 1775, inevitably dragging down prices.[13] This meant that, when merchants and planters in the Chesapeake drew bills of exchange on metropolitan merchants to be paid for out of the proceeds of consigned tobacco, they might well overdraw, for with falling prices their tobacco would not realize as much as expected a few months before. Moreover, since the tobacco trade provided a substantial proportion of London bills available in Scotland, a drop in the price of tobacco would have reduced the supply of London bills in Scotland and put pressure on all Scottish trading houses, particularly those that were most extended.

Such was the situation when the bubble burst in June 1772.[14] The Chesapeake and other American merchants in Britain were indebted to the warehousemen as never before because of the extraordinarily heavy shipments of goods in 1771 and the first half of 1772, most of which had not yet been paid for. In America there was a glut of European and Asian goods so that the importers found it hard to sell those on hand or to collect from the inland shopkeepers to whom they had sold parts of their earlier importations. And tobacco prices were falling in Europe as the 1772 crop in the fields showed every sign of being the third bumper crop in a row. (Prices stayed up in America a few months longer because of the great volume of shipping sent to the Chesapeake in the spring and summer of 1772, but this caused further losses since prices paid then in America could not be justified when the tobacco was resold in Europe.)

When the crisis hit London, there was no immediate panic among those merchants and warehousemen heavily involved in the American trades, because the amounts owing on twelve months' credit would only gradually become due in the course of the coming year.[15] However, the merchants sensed the panic psychology, and seeing all possible sources of external credit drying up at the banks and elsewhere, they became very cautious. Most of them soon began to refuse to accept bills of exchange not covered by effects in hand. With the fall in tobacco prices, such shortfalls in book credits were becoming increasingly common. However, the same relatively small group of merchants in each port on whom the bills were drawn were most often those to whom the bills were also payable. Thus the merchants increasingly pinched one another as they refused bill after bill. Joshua Johnson's records show that about 25 percent of the bills he received from America in the year starting August 1772 were refused and had to be returned protested (that is, with a notarial record of nonpayment). Other merchants, lacking Johnson's well-connected partners in the Chesapeake, may have had slightly higher proportions protested.

With something like 25 percent of bills of exchange being protested and tobacco prices continuing to fall, the Chesapeake merchants of Britain soon faced very serious liquidity problems. There was, however, no panic in this trade. The big warehousemen realized that they would gain nothing by driving their customers into bankruptcy, and they generally allowed everyone extensions of six additional months on twelve-month debts, only charging interest at 5 percent per annum for the extra months. Some smaller and weaker suppliers, who might have been in terribly straitened circumstances themselves, caused trouble, but they were not important enough to undermine the general solidity of credit.

The impression given by the merchants' correspondence is confirmed by the statistics of failures. Although published bankruptcies in the two years ending 30 September 1773 were 41 percent higher than in the two previous years,[16] little of this is ascribable to the Chesapeake trade. Only two identifiable houses trading to Virginia and Maryland went through formal bankruptcy proceedings as a direct result of the panic of 1772: Robert & Robert Bogle & Scott of London; and Simson, Baird & Company of Glasgow. As they were correspondents, their bankruptcies can almost be considered as one.[17] This trivial use of formal bankruptcy procedures was consistent with the recent history of the trade, if not with practices earlier in the century. Though the distress of 1711 forced many Chesapeake merchants to take advantage of the newly reorganized English bankruptcy procedures, there was thereafter a marked tendency to avoid this course (table 11).[18] In Scotland, the situation was much the same both before and after the reform of bankruptcy procedures in 1772. Since Chesapeake merchants had most of their effects outside the country, there was little point in dragging them into bankruptcy. The trade had its own more circumspect ways of handling sickly firms tottering on the edge of insolvency.

If the six months' extension of credit offered by the big warehousemen was not enough—as too often was the case in 1773—the experienced Chesapeake merchant called in his largest creditors and opened his books.[19] Two of the greatest firms in the London trade—James Russell and John Buchanan & Son, both heavily involved in the cargo trade—had to do this in 1773. Both probably had in the vicinity of £100,000 sterling owing them in America. Although their cases

Table 11. *Formal bankruptcies of English Chesapeake merchants, 1711–1770*

Decade	Number of firms
1711–1720	13
1721–1730	2
1731–1740	4
1741–1750	3
1751–1760	3
1761–1770	3

Source: PRO, Ind. 22634-53 (B.4/1-20), Court of Bankruptcy Docket Books.

were similar, their creditors reached different decisions. Perhaps because John Buchanan was so old (he was to die shortly afterward) and his only surviving son, Gilbert (who later became a clergyman) was so inexperienced, the creditors decided that the firm should be wound up even though its books showed assets exceeding liabilities by £50,000! In exchange for turning over all their assets to trustees named by the creditors and helping with collections, the Buchanans, father and son, were allowed £500 a year for living expenses during the winding-up period. In Russell's case, however, the greater vigor of the head of the firm (who in 1773, at sixty-five, went out to America himself to stimulate collections) and the influence of an extensive family connection in Britain and America induced the creditors to let the firm continue, though under the supervision of trustees for the creditors, who had to approve the payment of all bills of exchange and the dispatch of all future cargoes.

Lesser firms calling in their creditors might receive either the treatment of a Russell or that of a Buchanan. The young Christopher Court was allowed to continue, perhaps because of his connection with Thomas Eden, the brother of Governor Robert Eden of Maryland. Others were forced to wind up, including the possessors of old names in the Chesapeake trade: James Anderson, Thomas Philpot, and John Bland. Winding up meant turning over everything to trustees for one's creditors, but in the cases of Philpot and Anderson, "compositions" were arranged; when relatives of the merchant in difficulty agreed to countersign notes, all claims were settled for ten shillings in the pound or less. In one very complicated case, the big firm of Perkins, Buchanan & Brown appears to have turned over much of its business to its principal creditors, the wholesale linendrapers Barlow, Wigginton & Francis, who by 1775 had of necessity become Virginia merchants.

In all of this, there was not a single important failure among the warehousemen and other big suppliers, and the essential fabric of credit remained unshaken. The trade continued on the same lines down to the Revolution and was to resume on essentially the same lines after the war.

In the Chesapeake, the three levels of credit receivers described at the beginning of this chapter met the crisis of 1772 and the depression of 1772–1774 with different degrees of suffering. The small farmer found his income reduced by the fall in tobacco prices and his store debts harder to pay off. He could in some areas—within limits prescribed by his rent and tax obligations—switch part of his labor from tobacco to cereals. His ability to get additional credit was reduced although it was unlikely that he would be prosecuted for his old debts: they were usually too small.

Larger planters, by contrast, may well have felt themselves more threatened. Some could transfer part of their land to cereals, but the difficulties in using their slave labor force efficiently limited this option. (The very large tobacco crops of 1773 and 1774 suggest that there could not have been very much change in crops planted.) The larger planter's reduced income probably reduced the availability of credit for the purchase not just of luxuries but also of additional land and slaves. He would be put under increased pressure to cover some of his older debts by bonds or mortgages (he was rich enough to be sued), and he would find the fixed interest on his existing debt more burdensome as his income declined. Nevertheless, most in this class could, like the smaller farmers, get by through retrenchment and a postponement of slave and land purchases and improvements. Only in extreme cases would mortgages be foreclosed or land and slaves sold to meet court judgments or other debts.

Far more precarious was the position of the indigenous merchants in the Chesapeake, particularly those in the tobacco-growing regions. Unlike those neighbors, such as the merchants of Baltimore, who dealt primarily in wheat and flour and were sustained by good markets in Europe and relatively high prices throughout the early 1770s, the merchants in the tobacco-growing regions were sorely pressed. In the two years preceding the crash of June 1772 they had imported exceptionally large cargoes from Britain. A good portion of these goods was still on hand and was very difficult to sell in a time of glut. Much that was sold resulted only in book credits that were hard to realize as falling tobacco prices reduced the disposable resources of planters, farmers, and inland storekeepers. At the same time, these indigenous merchants were obliged to pay for their cargoes in twelve months and were charged interest after that time. If they were laggard in their remittances to Britain, they would find their bills of exchange protested, heavy penalties incurred, and their local credit undermined. They were under great pressure to sustain their remittances to Britain, not just to cover their bills of exchange but to help the merchants there whose credit was pledged on their cargoes. If one's correspondent in London failed, where would one find another correspondent in such times? What mercy could one expect from the trustees of his creditors? Many an indigenous merchant must have felt himself on the brink of ruin in the two years following the crash of 1772. Some were saved, at least for the moment, only by the closing of the courts in 1774.

It is incorrect to think of debt in the Chesapeake on the eve of the American Revolution as something owing only by planters to metropolitan merchants, or even by Americans to Britons. Aubrey Land has shown that the amount owed to local creditors far exceeded that owed to merchants and others in Britain.[20] Emory Evans has reviewed the entire question and concluded that debt has been considerably exaggerated as a cause of revolutionary unrest or protest.[21] Yet the economic distress that followed the crisis must have heightened the sense of unease fed from so many other sources. We do know that the tobacco-growing regions tended to be more revolutionary than the wheat-growing regions in the same states. (This is particularly striking in Maryland.) We also sense that the indigenous merchant class in the tobacco-growing regions (excluding Scottish factors and other foreign-born) was much more enthusiastically and consistently revolutionary than its counterpart farther north.[22]

The peace of 1783 left unresolved the rather intractable question of prewar debts, which kept diplomats on both sides busy for a generation and was not finally settled until the years 1802–1811. This controversy created a vast documentation, much of which survives in Public Record Office class T.79 (even though much more was probably destroyed at the Treasury in the nineteenth century). Justice can perhaps be done to this material only by some ambi-

tious program of computer analysis. A start has been
made by Richard Sheridan, who looked in particular
for the debtor position of members of the colonial
legislatures.[23] Of great interest for this study is the
distribution of the postwar debt among the three different credit levels or classes. At first glance one is
struck by the great mass of little men, small planters
and dirt farmers, owing, for example, £10 or less to
one of the Cuninghame stores, comparable to the
equivalent small debtors at indigenous stores reported
by Land.[24] Further examination reveals a sprinkling of
larger planters (who may or may not have been merchants also), as well as a significant number of accounts that were definitely mercantile. The debt that
was weighing down Jefferson in the 1780s was not his
own or his father's, but that of his father-in-law, the
merchant John Wayles, whose firm of Wayles & Randolph owed over £6,000 to Farell & Jones of Bristol.
Farell & Jones was also owed £3,361 by Jermyn Baker,
sometime merchant of Portsmouth (Virginia), and
£2,367 by Temple, Newsome & Wray of Petersburg.[25]
The claim of Matthias Gale, merchant of London, was
almost entirely against Virginia merchants, including
£2,033 against Roger Atkinson of Petersburg.[26] Atkinson also was listed for £1,164 in the largely mercantile
petition submitted by Samuel Lyde of London.[27]
Daniel Mildred's claim was against Edward Dorsey,
merchant, of Ann Arundel County, Maryland, and
Edward Stabler, merchant of Petersburg (a fellow
Quaker).[28] The claims of Samuel Gist of London were
also mercantile, including one for £5,281 against
Richard Booker & Company of Petersburg.[29] Whereas
Cuninghames concentrated on the small men of the
backcountry, the records of their Glasgow rivals,

Speirs & Company, with over £90,000 owing in 1777 at just four of its stores in Petersburg, Manchester, Osbornes (Chesterfield County), and Richmond, show a heavy intermixture of big merchant accounts.[30]

The picture in the post-1790 debt claims is confirmed by earlier evidence. During the Revolutionary War various states passed laws permitting local debtors owing money to British creditors to pay such debts into the state treasuries in depreciated wartime paper money. Debts could thus be paid off for $\frac{1}{40}$ of their prewar value. We have accounts of all the sums paid into the treasury of Maryland under this law. They show a striking preponderance of large debts owed by local traders to London merchants who had sent them cargoes before the war. Fully 75 percent of all sums paid into the treasury represented debts owing to six large London merchants, generous shippers of cargoes before the crisis of 1772. These show an even more striking preponderance of mercantile debt and an absence of planter debt.[31]

A full-scale study is needed of the changing economic and political fortunes of members of the indigenous merchant class in the Chesapeake before, during, and after the Revolution. Not only were they apparently the principal (indeed, almost the only) beneficiaries of the laws for paying British debts into the state treasuries, but they were also able to use depreciated paper money to pay off their other debts, including those to provincial loan offices. On the other hand, they had to accept this same paper from their own debtors and take equivalent losses.

8

The Implications for British Industrial and Commercial Development

FROM THE DETAILS of the exchange and credit relations that linked, step by step, the fabricator of goods in Britain with the overseas consumer, something approaching a normative model emerges. The cottage artisan or fabricator worked most commonly on some sort of putting-out arrangement for a clothier, iron manufacturer, or other merchant-manufacturer. As soon as the clothier or other manufacturer received the goods from the cottage artisan, he dispatched them to his factor in London, Bristol, or perhaps some other center. The factor helped finance the clothier (or other merchant-manufacturer) by furnishing him with raw materials on credit and by permitting the clothier to draw on him as soon as the goods were received, even though it might be many months before they were sold and still longer before they were paid for. If the factor was very affluent (as were the Fludyers, for example), he might then sell on long credits to the export merchant, who required credit of at least twelve months. More often, the factor appears to have sold on shorter credit to the warehouseman or other wholesaler to whom he shifted the burden of financing the export and much of the internal trade. (We know little or nothing about the precise relations between factor and warehouseman.) Just as the factor helped finance manufacture, so the warehouseman helped finance distribution by selling to the export merchant or internal trader with twelve or more months' credit. The export merchant exported the goods either on his own account (as did the Glasgow companies trading to the Chesapeake) or on order from abroad (as did the London commission merchants in the cargo and planter-consignment trades). The merchant or Glasgow store receiving the goods abroad might sell them retail or act as a wholesaler and pass them to inland retailers who sold them to the ultimate consumer.

Not every article followed precisely this course. Foreign linens may sometimes have been sold on credit by the factor, cutting out the warehouseman (wholesale linendraper). Sometimes the export merchant or warehouseman ordered goods directly from the putting-out manufacturer, cutting out the factor. Sometimes warehousemen might export goods on their own, cutting out the export merchant; provincial merchants and manufacturers might export goods entirely on their own, cutting out both factors and warehousemen in London or other big ports. Nevertheless, something like the model given can be fairly described as normative. Its most striking feature was the strategic importance of capital mobilization. It was the superiority of the factor as a capital mobilizer that gave him his strong position vis-à-vis the clothier or other merchant-manufacturer. It was the superiority of the warehouseman (wholesale linendraper, wholesale ironmonger, and the like) as a capital mobilizer that made him so indispensable to the export merchant. Other nations, including the Dutch, had different trading systems; but it was the strong wholesaler offering credits of twelve months and upward who characteristically financed much of British export trade as it existed in the eighteenth century.

Although we know little about factors and warehousemen-wholesalers, the scraps of information available suggest that like other traders they mobilized capital partly by inheritance and marriage, partly by plowing back profits, and partly by borrowing on bond or note from those who wished a higher rate of interest than was available (after Walpole's time) from government securities or mortgages. (T. S. Ashton has emphasized the importance of the lower interest rates on government stock during the mid-eighteenth century in diverting savings toward investment in turnpike and canal companies.[1] The same phenomenon may have diverted millions in savings toward the higher yield of the commercial and industrial sectors, particularly via the bond market.) While the export merchant inevitably had most of his effects (goods and credits) abroad, the factor and warehouseman usually held their effects at home as stock on hand and as credits owing from persons in Great Britain. Thus they probably appeared to be better risks than export merchants, and, other things being equal, they had less trouble in attracting loans on bonds or notes: hence their greater effectiveness as capital mobilizers.

It is probably no accident that some of the great banking fortunes of the nineteenth century had their origins in eighteenth century business firms not trading abroad but operating primarily at home as factors or warehousemen: wholesale linendrapers like Barclays and Paynes of London and Wilsons of Leeds; mercers like Smiths of Nottingham, dealers in woolen yarn like the Gurneys, or wholesale ironmongers like the Lloyds of Birmingham. It was firms of this sort that were most successful in mobilizing capital in the eighteenth century and that therefore found it easiest to branch out into banking.

The preexistence of this normative chain of trade and credit must have facilitated the earlier stages of the industrial revolution. The early innovating manufacturers found merchant firms already in existence that were accustomed to providing raw materials on credit and also accustomed to taking manufactured goods on consignment for sale with partial payment (by accepting bills of exchange) long before sale. However, as the new manufacturing firms grew, they may have found the dependent role ascribed to the manufacturer by the old system rather irksome. There were too many middlemen between the manufacturer and the ultimate consumer. Though the credits offered by these middlemen encouraged manufacture and distribution, their profits and commissions tended to raise prices and ultimately to discourage consumption. The long credits too resulted in a somewhat cumbersome system with capital turning over rather slowly. At some point, it would seem that the disadvantages of the old system began to outweigh the advantages in the minds of some manufacturers. In the post-1815 years, some of the newer-style manufacturers succeeded in breaking out of the old arrangements completely. In their pioneer but still valuable studies, R. B.

Westerfield and N. S. Buck describe a markedly different system of British-American trade operating in the decades after 1815.

First of all, Buck's evidence from the 1820s indicates that credits in foreign trade had recently shrunk from over twelve to about six months. He does not explain this change, but the fact that the adjustment occurred during the bank suspension period (1797–1820) leads one to speculate that the increased paper money supply may have eased the cash problems of buyers even while inflation made sellers reluctant to continue assuming the enhanced risks of traditional long credits.

In the second place, Buck and Westerfield describe a structurally different trade in which the British textile manufacturer frequently shipped goods on his own account to commission merchants in New York and other American ports with instructions to sell immediately by auction for cash and remit the proceeds.[2] In this way, the manufacturer apparently disposed of surplus stocks, kept his factory operating more fully than he otherwise could have, realized some economies of scale and full operation, and improved his cash position. Though the prices received at auction must frequently have been disappointing, the manufacturers in their own way apparently appreciated the difference not only between cash and credit prices but also between average and marginal costs, and calculated that they were not losing by such prices. The consignment-to-auction system was not characteristic of British export trade generally, and even in the U.S. trade its major impact seems to have been confined to the years 1815–1840. Nevertheless, the existence of such a system at that time suggests that British manufacturers had gained access to sufficient resources (both capital and longer-term credit) to free them from total dependence on the port commission merchants and warehousemen—but not enough to permit them to offer the long credits formerly extended by warehousemen. This is a problem that is now beginning to attract the serious attention it deserves.[3]

Interestingly enough, there is evidence that the auction system was used for selling European manufactures in North America from the 1740s on. Although we do not find such auctions in the Chesapeake before the Revolution, we do find frequent traces of them about 1748–1775 in Charleston, New York, and Philadelphia; and some of the auctioned goods were even then sent directly from Manchester. However, such auctions appear almost always to have been emergency measures used to dispose of goods that could not be sold in the normal way within the time constraints of the British consignor or American importer. As such they were but unwilling experiments until at least the 1780s.[4] The typical British merchant-manufacturer before the American Revolution, with his limited resources and aversion to risk, was still tied to the factor and warehouseman for the disposal of his goods. They and their credit offered a marketing service quite effective for its time.

The Chesapeake trade was noteworthy in the eighteenth century for the duration of the credits it required. Long credits inevitably meant higher totals of debts outstanding at any given moment in proportion to sales. But there was nothing peculiar about an eighteenth century British trade being based on credit, nor was there anything peculiar to the Chesapeake in the British institutions that supported this credit. Much more research needs to be done, but the present fragmentary evidence suggests that the Chesapeake trade's dependence on credit was not untypical of contemporary British export trades to North America, the West Indies, and parts of southern Europe.

Appendixes
Notes
Bibliography
Index

Markups and Profit Margins in the Chesapeake Trade

T *HE PRECISE MARKUPS* and profit margins used in the Chesapeake trade are obscure. Their obscurity is rendered more impenetrable by contemporary usage, which combined the markup and the conversion into local currency into a single calculation called the "advance," based on the British cost of the goods shown in the bill of sale (bill of parcels, shop note) of the warehouseman or other supplier and excluding the freight and insurance that had to come out of the profit margin. Hence, Joshua Johnson could say that fluctuations in exchange could wipe out the profits on goods sold at "an advance of 100."[1] He was in fact referring to a transaction similar to that shown in the first row of the following table on advances, in which British goods sold in Maryland at wholesale received a 20 percent markup and were then converted into Maryland currency (at 1.667 to 1) for a total advance of 100—or, alternatively, to one in which goods were sold at a 25 percent markup and converted into Maryland currency at 1.6 to 1 for the same total advance. In either case a "rise in exchange" (that is, a rise in the price of sterling) of about 15 percentage points (such as occurred in 1770–1771) could eliminate almost half the gross gain in the advance, and much of the rest would be consumed by freight and insurance (about 2.5 percent each) and by other operating expenses.

In interpreting contemporary references it is important to keep in mind this dual nature of the advance and not to count as and incorporate into profits what are only conversions from one mone-

Advances on £100 sterling worth of British goods, incorporating both markups and monetary conversions.

Sterling markup or advance	Sterling sale price	Converted to Maryland currency at par (166.7:100)	Converted to Virginia currency at par (125:100)
20%	£120	£200 (100 advance)	£150 (50 advance)
50	150	250 (150 advance)	187.10.0 (87.5 advance)
80	180	300 (200 advance)	225 (125 advance)

tary system to another. It would appear that markups for wholesale transactions for cash or early payment were usually about 20 percent and sometimes might be as little as 10 percent on strictly cash transactions. Markups for retail sales for cash or early payment in port towns would appear to have been in the vicinity of 50 percent, while markups on indefinite credit sales in interior stores might have ranged up to 80 percent.[2]

Capitalization of Glasgow Chesapeake Firms between 1740 and 1789 (*in Sterling*)

Firm	Date	Capital[a]	Reference
Andrew Aiton & Co.	ca. 1740	ca. £6,575 (*s,a,e*)	SRA, B10/15, nos. 5483, 5519, 5528
John Alston & Co.	1767	12,000 (*p*)	PRO, T.79/22
(successor firm: *Alston, Young & Co.*)	1774–75	26,850 (*b*)	PRO, T.79/33(10)
Baird, Hay & Co.	1772	10,000 (*b*)	SRA, T-MJ 79
	1777	15,994 (*b*)	SRA, T-MJ 79
John Ballantine & Co.	1776	13,588 (*b*)	PRO, T.79/31
John Barns & Co.	1757	3,000 (*p*)	SRA, B10/15, no. 7036
Bogle, Brown & Co.	1774	2,500 (*c*)	Mitchell Library, Steggall-Bogle MSS, XCI(ii), p. 29

Firm	Date	Quantity	Source
Bogles, Cross & Co.	1763	2,930 *(i,e)*	SRO, CC9/7/65, pp. 195–199
Bogle, Somervell & Co.	1768	6,500 *(p)*	SRA, B10/15, no. 8045
	1776	16,640 *(s,e)*	SRA, B10/15, no. 8045
John Bogle & Co.	1750	ca. 12,500 *(s,e)*	SRO, CC9/16/56
(successor firm: *Patrick & William*			
Bogle & Co.)	1763	11,187 *(i,e)*	SRO, CC9/7/65, pp. 195–199
Buchanan, Hastie & Co.			
(main concern)	1763	10,500 *(p)*	SRA, B10/12/4, fols. 28v–32v
	1774	23,014 *(b)*	PRO, T.79/25
	1775	16,385 *(b)*	PRO, T.79/25
(Nansemond concern)	1770	10,000 *(p)*	SRA, B10/12/4, fols. 28v–32v
			SRO, CC9/16/75 (23.vi.1778)
Buchanan & Simson	Jan. 1759	12,000 *(p)*	SRO, CC9/16/54 (3.viii.1762)
	Dec. 1759	15,200 *(b)*	SRO, C.S.96/506/1
	Dec. 1760	18,400 *(b)*	SRO, C.S.96/506/1
	Dec. 1761	17,200 *(b)*	SRO, C.S.96/506/1
	Dec. 1762	19,200 *(b)*	SRO, C.S.96/504–505
	Aug. 1764	19,200 *(b)*	SRO, C.S.96/504–505
	1753	16,200 *(p)*	SRA, B10/15, no. 6653
Buchanan, Speirs & Co.[b]	1768	8,000	Devine, *Tobacco Lords*, 75
G. & A. Buchanan & Co.	1755	13,582 *(i,e)*	SRO, CC9/7/63, pp. 274–275
Cochrane, Crawford & Co.			
(successor firm: *Cochrane,*	1765	20,692 *(i,e)*	SRO, CC9/7/65, pp. 453–455
Cuninghame & Co.)	Mar. 1773	72,000 *(p)*	SRO, RD3/309, pp. 58–81
(successor firm: *Wm. Cuninghame &*	June 1773	79,200 *(p)*	PRO, T.79/1
Co.)			

Firm	Date	Capital[a]	Reference
Cochrane, Murdoch & Co.	ca. 1755	£22,903 (*i,e*)	SRO, CC9/7/63, pp. 275–276
	ca. 1760	26,400 (*i,e*)	SRO, CC9/7/64, pp. 42–48
		23,185 (*s,e*)	SRO, CC9/7/64, pp. 99–103
Alexander Cuninghame & Co.	1770	15,000 (*p*)	SRA, B10/15, no. 7606
(after 1772, Cuninghame, Findlay & Co.)	1771	11,817 (*b*)	Signet Library, Session Papers, 162/23
	1772	11,672 (*b*)	Signet Library, Session Papers, 162/23
James & Robert Donald & Co.	ca. 1760	23,262 (*i,e*)	SRO, CC9/7/64, pp. 42–48
		18,953 (*s,e*)	SRO, CC9/7/64, pp. 35–39, CC9/16/58 (18.vii.1765)
	1772	75,000 (*b*)	PRO, T.79/15
	1773	65,000 (*b*)	PRO, T.79/15
Donald, Scot & Co.	1776	38,226 (*b*)	PRO, T.79/18
Findlay, Hopkirk & Co.	1785	8,400 (*p*)	SRO, C.S.96/2240
	1787	15,917 (*b*)	SRO, C.S.96/2240
	1788	22,205 (*b*)	SRO, C.S.96/2240
	1789	21,055 (*b*)	SRO, C.S.96/2240
Glassford, Gordon, Monteath & Co.	1771	24,000 (*p*)	PRO, T.79/26
John Graham & Co.	1759	3,000 (*p*)	SRO, CC9/16/60 (24.iv.1767)
Henderson, McCall & Co.	1771	35,000 (*c*)	LC, Jamieson MSS, XIV, fol. 3113
McCall, Dennistoun & Co.	1775	13,476 (*b*)	PRO, T.79/15, fol. 257
McCall & Elliot (Va. concern)	1766	12,000 (*p*)	SRA, B10/15, no. 8269
McCall, Elliot & Co. (N.C. concern)	1771	4,000 (*p*)	SRA, B10/15, no. 8270
McCall, Smellie & Co.	1767	18,376 (*b*)	PRO, T.79/11
John McCall & Co.	1769	10,000 (*p*)	SRA, B10/15, no. 8123

Firm	Year	Value	Source
John M'Dowall & Co.	1769	4,000	House of Lords appeal
Jas. Murdoch & Thos. Yuill	ca. 1747	6,500 (b)	SRA, B10/15, no. 5888
George Pagan & Co.	1761	2,000 (p)	SRA, T-MJ 422
Ramsay, Monteath & Co.	1772	6,500 (p)	PRO, T.79/27
Smith, Scott & Co.	1742	2,400 (p)	Lanarkshire Sheriff Court (4.i.1742)
Alexander Speirs & Co.	1761	£74,250 (a,e)	SRO, CC9/16/53
(successor firm: Speirs, Bowman & Co.)	1765	90,350 (i,e)	SRO, CC9/7/65, pp. 491–492
	1770	153,172 (b,e)	SRA, TD131/6/1
	1771	158,261 (b,e)	SRA, TD131/6/1
	1772	162,071 (b,e)	SRA, TD131/4
	1773	153,569 (b,e)	SRA, TD131/4
		152,280 (p)	PRO, T.79/11
	1774	151,804 (b,e)	SRA, TD131/4
	1775	172,245 (b,e)	SRA, TD131/4
	1776	196,676 (b,e)	SRA, TD131/4
Speirs, Mackie & Co.	1765	6,240 (i,e)	SRO, CC9/7/65, pp. 491–492
(successor firm: Speirs, French & Co.)	1770	22,251 (b,e)	SRA, TD131/61
	1771	27,577 (b,e)	SRA, TD131/4
	1773	23,076 (b,e)	SRA, TD131/4
	1779	55,872 (b,e)	SRA, TD131/4
Thomson, Snodgrass & Co.	1776	10,000 (p)	SRA, B10/12/4, fols. 124–127v
Wylie, Muirhead & Co.	1770	1,500 (p)	PRO, T.79/6, fols. 46–49

a. Code letters indicating nature of underlying evidence: *a*, arbitration valuation of share; *b*, value in firm's (or partner's) books or other accounts; *c*, correspondence; *e*, estimate from valuation of one partner's share; *i*, inventory valuation of share; *p*, partnership contract or sederunt book supplement; *s*, sale value of share.

b. See Alexander Speirs & Co. and Speirs, Mackie & Co. for successor firms.

Document on Credit and the Cargo Trade

Circular letter sent by Farell & Jones of Bristol to sixteen mercantile correspondents in Virginia, 10 August 1770, specifying the terms on which they would carry on the cargo trade. PRO, T.79/30 (Farell & Jones claim).

As we find that the Merchants in general of London Liverpool etc. do now purchase their Goods [for American correspondents] at 12 Months Credit and that it would be more agreeable to our [mercantile] Friends in Virginia if we did the same we have determined to conform thereto and take this Opportunity to inform you the Terms on which we propose doing Business in future with you and our other [mercantile] Corrispondents to prevent any mistakes between us viz. We will purchase Goods [ordered by you] at twelve Months Credit and allow you the same [length of credit]. If we are not in Cash [received from you] at the End of twelve Months we are to charge Interest whilst in advance after the rate of five p[er] Cent p[er] Annum[;] if you remit ready Money or [commodities] before the [payments for] the Goods are due we will allow you a Discount thereon after the same Rate[,] the full Remittance to be made by you once a Year [that is, by year's end] or sooner if agreeable to you either in Bills or Tobacco[,] if in the latter we will give you Credit for the freight charged on your Goods by our own ships to the Amount of the nett Proceeds of your Tobacco, but for what we may happen to ship on other Peoples Vessels we can make no Allowance as we must pay the freight out of our own Pockets and of course it would take away the whole of our Commissions. And lastly as we have sometimes been obliged to pay an Attorney [in Virginia] five p[er] Cent to recover Debts from Gentlemen when they drop Correspondence with us besides losing Interest thereon from the time the Debt is paid in Virginia to the times the Bills become due here frequently five or six Months—therefore whenever a Gentleman declines Correspondence with us, he is to pay the Balance of Account into our Compting House with Interest thereon to the time we are in Cash here free from all Charges as we may be put to in recovering the same—We dare say you will think these terms just and reasonable on both sides and if you choose to continue your Correspondence with us thereon we entreat you will sign your Consent at the foot hereof for Mr. Evans to transmitt to us and keep a Duplicate—signed by us in order to prevent any Mistakes on either side in this respect at least in future Correspondence.

British-Chesapeake Trade, 1669-1776

Year	British tobacco imports (in thousands of lbs. wt.)[a]			British exports to Chesapeake (in thousands of £ sterling)[a]		
	England	Scotland	Britain	England	Scotland	Britain
1669[b]	15,040	—	—	—	—	—
1672	17,559	—	—	—	—	—
1682	21,399	—	—	—	—	—
1686[b]	28,036	—	—	—	—	—
1687[b]	27,567	—	—	—	—	—
1688[b]	28,385	—	—	—	—	—
1694	27,837	—	—	—	—	—
1697[b]	35,632	—	—	£59	—	—
1698[b]	23,052	—	—	310	—	—

Year					
	—	—			
	—	—			
1699			31,253	—	205
1700			37,840	—	173
1701			32,194	—	200
1702			37,209	—	72
1703			20,075	—	197
1704			34,864	—	60
1705			15,661	—	174
1706			19,763	—	58
1707			28,088	—	238
1708			28,975	1,449^c	30,424	79
1709			34,547	1,449^c	35,997	80
1710			23,498	1,449^c	24,947	128
1711			28,121	1,449^d	29,571	92
1712			30,523	—	—	£135
1713			21,598	—	—	76
1714			29,264	—	—	129
1715			17,810	2,449^d	20,259	199
1716			28,316	2,449^d	30,765	180
1717			29,600	2,449^d	32,049	216
1718			31,840	—	—	192
1719			33,684	—	—	165
1720			34,526	—	—	111
1721			37,292	4,090^b	41,382	127
1722			28,542	6,720^b	35,261	173

| | British tobacco imports (in thousands of lbs. wt.)[a] | | | British exports to Chesapeake (in thousands of £ sterling)[a] | | |
Year	England	Scotland	Britain	England	Scotland	Britain
1723	29,295	4,783[b]	34,078	124	—	—
1724	26,634	5,717[b]	32,351	162	—	—
1725	21,047	4,193[b]	25,239	196	—	—
1726	32,311	3,858[b]	36,169	186	—	—
1727	43,275	6,972[b]	50,247	193	—	—
1728	42,588	7,234[b]	49,821	171	—	—
1729	39,951	7,192[b]	47,143	109	—	—
1730	35,080	5,526[b]	40,606	151	—	—
1731	41,595	4,096[b]	45,691	171	—	—
1732	30,891	—	—	148	—	—
1733	40,085	—	—	186	—	—
1734	35,563	—	—	172	—	—
1735	40,069	—	—	220	—	—
1736	37,904	—	—	£205	—	—
1737	50,208	—	—	211	—	—
1738	40,120	4,588	44,708	259	—	—
1739	46,724	6,643	53,367	217	—	—
1740	36,002	5,303	41,305	281	£75	£357
1741	59,449	8,925	68,374	249	73	321
1742	43,467	9,739	53,206	264	93	357

1743	56,767	10,627	67,394	328	121	449
1744	41,434	10,727	52,161	235	78	313
1745	41,073	13,612	54,686	198	87	284
1746	39,990	11,729	51,719	283	148	431
1747	51,289	12,757	64,045	200	163	363
1748	50,695	16,922	67,617	253	166	418
1749	44,648	22,315	66,964	324	94	418
1750	51,339	19,688	71,027	349	109	458
1751	45,979	20,914	66,893	347	131	478
1752	57,250	21,569	78,820	325	133	458
1753	62,686	21,524	84,210	357	127	484
1754	58,867	17,772	76,387	324	106	430
1755	49,084	15,810	64,894	285	99	385
1756	33,291	12,214	45,505	335	88	423
1757	42,232	17,860	60,092	427	102	529
1758	43,969	25,693	69,662	438	108	547
1759	34,782	14,886	49,668	459	112	571
1760	52,347	32,183	84,530	£606	£155	£761
1761	47,075	26,262	73,337	545	132	678
1762	44,111	26,708	70,819	418	125	542
1763	65,179	32,839	98,018	555	196	751
1764	54,443	26,347	80,790	515	174	689
1765	48,320	33,160	81,479	383	136	519
1766	43,318	29,344	72,663	373	147	520
1767	39,145	28,938	68,083	438	215	653

Year	British tobacco imports (in thousands of lbs. wt.)[a]			British exports to Chesapeake (in thousands of £ sterling)[a]		
	England	Scotland	Britain	England	Scotland	Britain
1768	35,555	33,237	68,792	476	194	670
1769	33,797	36,303	70,100	488	227	715
1770	39,188	38,709	77,897	718	279	997
1771	58,093	47,269	105,362	920	303	1,224
1772	51,502	45,260	96,762	794	222	1,016
1773	55,936	44,543	100,479	429	161	589
1774	56,057	41,348	97,405	529	161	690
1775	55,969	45,863	101,832	2	0	2
1776	7,275	7,423	14,698	0	0	0

Sources: For tobacco imports: PRO, Customs 2, 3, 14, and 17; PRO, C.O.388/2, fol. 13 (1669); Earl of Lonsdale's muniments (1669); Gray & Wyckoff (1672, 1682); BL, Sloane MS 1815, fols. 34–37 (1686–1688); House of Lords parchment collection (1694); PRO, C.O.390/5/47 (1703–1720, Eng.); PRO, T.1/139/29 (1708–1711, Scot.); PRO, C.O.390/5/13 (1715–1717, Scot.); PRO, T.1/282/23 (1721–1724, Scot.); PRO, T.36/13 (1725–1731, Scot.); PRO, T.1/329, fol. 125 (1738–1747, Scot.); Clements Library, Townshend MSS (1749–1755, Scot.); SRO, E.504, 1748 and 1763; PRO, T.64/276B/328, 332 (1763–1773). For British exports: Jacob M. Price, "New Time Series for Scotland's and Britain's Trade with the Thirteen Colonies and States, 1740 to 1791," *William and Mary Quarterly*, 3d ser., 32 (1975), 320–321, 324–325; *Historical Statistics of the United States* (1976), II, 1176–78, reversing export/import designations (typographical error) in series Z, 227–244.

a. Figures rounded to nearest thousand.

b. Year ending at Michaelmas. Other years end at Christmas through 1751 and on 5 January from 1752.

c. Average of several years.

d. Average of several years ending at Michaelmas.

Notes

1 INTRODUCTION

1. There is relatively little on merchants and commercial credit in François Crouzet, ed., *Capital Formation in the Industrial Revolution* (London, 1972), but see ch. 2 by Herbert Heaton and ch. 6 by Sidney Pollard. There is only one sentence on the topic in Stanley D. Chapman, *The Early Factory Masters: The Transition to the Factory System in the Midlands Textile Industry* (Newton Abbot, 1967), 127; there is hardly more in Seymour Shapiro, *Capital and the Cotton Industry* (Ithaca, N.Y., 1967). Much more helpful is the treatment in Michael M. Edwards, *The Growth of the British Cotton Trade, 1780–1815* (Manchester, 1967), ch. 10. Cf. also Peter Mathias, "Capital, Credit and Enterprise in the Industrial Revolution," *Journal of European Economic History,* 2 (1973), 121–124. The argument that working capital was relatively more important (than fixed capital) in the eighteenth century than in later centuries is criticized in Philip E. Mirowski, "The Birth of the Business Cycle" (Ph.D. diss., University of Michigan, 1979), 445–450.

2. For some suggestions on the wealth of late seventeenth and early eighteenth century merchants, see R. Grassby, "English Merchant Capitalism in the Late Seventeenth Century: The Composition of Business Fortunes," *Past & Present,* no. 46 (1970), 87–107; idem, "The Personal Wealth of the Business Community in Seventeenth Century England," *Economic History Review,* 2d ser., 23 (1970), 220–234; D. W. Jones, "London Overseas-Merchant

Groups at the End of the Seventeenth Century and the Moves against the East India Company" (D.Phil. diss., Oxford, 1970), esp. 173–261; Jacob M. Price, *The Tobacco Adventure to Russia, Transactions of the American Philosophical Society,* n.s., 51, pt. 1 (Philadelphia, 1961), 105–109; J. R. Woodhead, *The Rulers of London 1660–1689* (London, 1965).

2 THE PROBLEM OF DEBT VIEWED FROM THE CHESAPEAKE

1. Jefferson's answer to Demeusnier's queries for the *Encyclopédie Méthodique,* in Julian P. Boyd, ed., *The Papers of Thomas Jefferson* (Princeton, N.J., 1950–), X, 27 (also 304–305).

2. The figure of three-fifths or more was obtained by assuming that all of the tobacco imported into Scotland (44 percent of British imports in 1764–1775) and about 32.5 percent of the remaining 56 percent going to England went on British merchants' account. This is a very conservative estimate, since as early as 1733, when Scotland accounted for only 13 percent of the trade, it was reported that "more than one half of the Importation of Tobacco from *Virginia* is on the proper Account of the Merchants of *Great Britain* trading to that Colony." *Considerations Relating to the Tobacco Trade at London, so Far as It Relates to the Merchants Who Are Factors* ([London, 1733]). If all the Scottish imports were on British merchants' account, then it would follow that at least 42.5 percent of the tobacco imported into *England* in 1733 was also on British merchants' account. I have reduced this 42.5 percent to 32.5 for the prewar calculation because the proportion of the *English* trade handled by the outports (centers of the direct trading system) declined from 39.2 percent in the period 1738–1743 to 29.8 percent in the period 1771–1773. Cf. Jacob M. Price, *France and the Chesapeake: A History of the French Tobacco Monopoly 1674–1791,* 2 vols. (Ann Arbor, Mich., 1973), I, 589–590.

3. For evidence of the use of simple interest in preparing debt claims in the 1780s, see PRO, A.O.13/27 (W. Bogle), A.O.13/30 (J. Glassford & Co.), A.O.13/33 (Donald, Scott & Co.), A.O.13/90 (Bogle, Somervell & Co.), and A.O.13/91 (W. Miller).

4. Cf. Edward C. Papenfuse, *In Pursuit of Profit: The Annapolis Merchants in the Era of the American Revolution, 1763–1805* (Baltimore, Md., 1975), 170–172; J. M. Price, "One Family's Empire: The Russell-Lee-Clerk Connection in Maryland, Britain and India,

1707–1857," *Maryland Historical Magazine*, 72 (1977), 203, 211–212.

5. David Macpherson, *Annals of Commerce*, III (London, 1805), 581. Merchants who wished to reestablish credit in Britain after the war had to settle their debts. Relatively few planters felt so obliged. Isaac S. Harrell, "Some Neglected Phases of the Revolution in Virginia," *William and Mary Quarterly*, 2d ser., 5 (1925), 169.

6. Richard Champion, *Considerations on the Present Situation of Great Britain and the United States of America*, 2d ed. (London, 1784), 269n.

7. Population data are from U.S. Bureau of the Census, *Historical Statistics of the United States, Colonial Times to 1957* (Washington, D.C., 1960), 756; idem, *Historical Statistics of the United States, Colonial Times to 1970*, 2 vols. (Washington, D.C., 1976), II, 1168. Trade data are from Jacob M. Price, "New Time Series for Scotland's and Britain's Trade with the Thirteen Colonies and States, 1740 to 1791," *William and Mary Quarterly*, 3d ser., 32 (1975), 324–325.

8. For the importance of credit in the Chesapeake before 1740, see William and Mary College Library, Williamsburg, Va., Jerdone Papers, William Johnston's Ledger F and Letterbook, Johnston to N. Buchanan, 16 Oct. 1738.

9. PRO, P.R.O.30/8/95, James Buchanan et al. to W. Pitt, 6 Jan. 1757; John C. Rainbolt, *From Prescription to Persuasion: Manipulation of Eighteenth Century Virginia Economy* (Port Washington, N.Y., 1974), 47, 86.

10. BL, Add. MSS 33,030, fols. 160v–162, 215.

11. Mitchell Library, Glasgow, Steggall-Bogle Papers, Journal of John Brown of Westerhaughs, I, 112–113.

12. See appendix D, and Price, "New Time Series," 320–321.

13. There is also a little evidence that Virginia and Maryland did not reduce their debt to Britain between 1774 and 1776 as much as Champion suggested that all the colonies did. For example, accounts of the firm John Ballantine & Co. of Glasgow show a reduction of about one-third between August 1774 and August 1775 in both debts owing in Virginia and net investment in Virginia. PRO, T.79/31. This might suggest that if the colonies as a whole (per Champion) reduced their British debt by two-thirds in the last year, Virginia only reduced its by one-third.

14. There are no readily available data on household size in eighteenth century Virginia. In Maryland, household size rose

from 6.8 (or 7.3), including slaves, in 1704 to 9.6 at the census of 1790. Assuming a constant rate of growth, I get an average household of ca. 8.6 in 1776, which I have extended to Virginia. Cf. Robert V. Wells, *The Population of the British Colonies in America before 1776* (Princeton, N.J., 1975), 156 and note; U.S. Bureau of the Census, *A Century of Population Growth . . . 1790–1900* (Washington, D.C., 1909), 288.

15. John McCusker, in order to convert English exports from official to current prices, prepared an "English wholesale commodity price index, 1697 to 1800" based on the earlier Schumpeter-Gilboy price indices. See his article, "The Current Value of English Exports, 1697 to 1800," *William and Mary Quarterly*, 3d ser., 28 (1971), 607–628, esp. 619–620. In his index, with 100 the average for 1700–1702, the average for 1765–1774 was 100.7! In between, the index fluctuated between 80 and 118 but went above 101.1 only twice. If one prefers not to use the McCusker index because it includes too many items not normally shipped from Britain to America, one can use instead the Schumpeter-Gilboy index for "consumer goods other than cereals." B. R. Mitchell and Phyllis Deane, *Abstract of British Historical Statistics* (Cambridge, 1962), 468–469. Here we find a slight decline in the index from 102.8 in 1700–1702 to 96.4 in 1765–1774. In between, the index never drops below 85 or (except on one occasion) goes above 104.

16. For examples of the importance of credit in the sale of European goods in Charleston and New York, see Philip M. Hamer, ed., *The Papers of Henry Laurens*, 7 vols. (Columbia, S.C., 1968–1979), I, 101, IV, 97, 185; Philip L. White, ed., *The Beekman Mercantile Papers, 1746–1799*, 3 vols. (New York, 1956), I, 92, 287–288, 350, 478. For the importance of credit in the West India trade, see D. W. Thoms, "The Mills Family: London Sugar Merchants of the Eighteenth Century," *Business History*, 11 (1969), 7–10; Richard Pares, *A West India Fortune* (London, 1950), ch. 11; idem, "A London West-India Merchant House, 1740–1769," in R. Pares and A. J. P. Taylor, eds., *Essays Presented to Sir Lewis Namier* (London, 1956), 98–107; idem, *Merchants and Planters, Economic History Review Supplement*, 4 (Cambridge, 1960), ch. 4; Richard B. Sheridan, *Sugar and Slavery: An Economic History of the British West Indies, 1623–1775* (Baltimore, Md., 1974), ch. 12.

17. PRO, T. 79/30, Wayles to Farell & Jones, 30 Aug. 1766.

18. See E. James Ferguson, "Currency Finance: An Interpretation of Colonial Monetary Practices," *William and Mary Quarterly*, 3d ser., 10 (1953), 153–180; Joseph A. Ernst, "Genesis of the Currency Act of 1764: Virginia Paper Money and the Protection of British Investments," ibid., 22 (1965), 33–74; Emory G. Evans, "Planter Indebtedness and the Coming of the Revolution in Virginia," ibid., 19 (1962), 511–533; Richard B. Sheridan, "The British Credit Crisis of 1772 and the American Colonies," *Journal of Economic History*, 20 (1960), 161–186.

3 CAPITALIZATION OF MERCHANT FIRMS

1. On the Jeffreys, see *Burke's Peerage* under "Lord Camden"; and Theophilus Jones, *A History of the County of Brecknock*, ed. Sir Joseph Russell Bailey and Edwin Davies, 4 vols. (Brecknock, 1909–1930), II, 143–144; J. R. Woodhead, ed., *The Rulers of London, 1660–1689* (London, 1965), 97–98. On Maurice Thompson, see Robert Brenner's long-awaited book.

2. See LC, Custis Papers, J. Hanbury to Col. J. Custis, 7 Mar. 1745/6. (I am indebted to John M. Hemphill for this reference.) On Perry, see E. M. Donnan, "Eighteenth Century Merchants: Micajah Perry," *Journal of Economic and Business History*, 4 (1931), 70–98; and Sir William Purdie Treloar, *A Lord Mayor's Diary, 1906–7 to Which is Added the Official Diary of Micajah Perry Lord Mayor, 1738–9* (London, 1920). On hints of Perry's stock in trade, see *The Free Briton*, 5 Apr. 1733.

3. MdHR, Joshua Johnson letterbook (Private Accounts 1507), p. 446, to firm, 4 Aug. 1774; printed version in Jacob M. Price, ed., *Joshua Johnson's Letterbook, 1771–1774: Letters from a Merchant in London to His Partners in Maryland*, London Record Society, XV (London, 1979), no. 157a.

4. On this family, see Amy A. Locke, *The Hanbury Family*, 2 vols. (London, 1916), II, esp. 232, 248–252.

5. MdHS, Hollyday MSS, W. Anderson to J. Hollyday, 6 Sept. 1758.

6. On the Glasgow fortunes, see T. M. Devine, *The Tobacco Lords: A Study of the Tobacco Merchants of Glasgow and Their Trading Activities* (Edinburgh, 1975), esp. chs. 1–7.

7. London Corporation RO, Orphans' inventories, box 37 (19

May 1701), and box 39 (7 June 1705). John Cary would appear to have also had ca. £4,500 invested in the firm of Peter Paggen & Co., big slave traders. For Trott, see PRO, Prob.4/2729.

8. PRO, C.O.5/1305/29, fols. 79–86.

9. [Fairfax Harrison], *The Devon Carys,* 2 vols. (New York, 1920), II, 680–684; PRO, P.C.C. 58 Dyer (John Cary) and 188 Fox (Thomas Cary); J. M. Price, "Who Was John Norton?" *William and Mary Quarterly,* 3d ser., 19 (1962), 400–407.

10. Colonial Williamsburg Foundation, Williamsburg, Va., Norton MSS, no. 17, John Norton to J. H. Norton, 4 Sept. 1773. In addition to the contracted "stock" of the firm, John Norton had advanced additional funds of his own on loan.

11. PRO, Prob. 11/840 (P.C.C. 257 Hutton), will of James Buchanan.

12. Price, ed., *Joshua Johnson's Letterbook,* nos. 74, 75, to C. Wallace, 10 Apr. 1773, and to firm, 12 Apr. 1773.

13. Ibid., no. 6, Johnson to firm, 26 July 1771.

14. See ibid., introduction.

15. Muniments of Sir James Hunter Blair, Bart., Ledger and Journal of Sir James Hunter Blair, 1st Bart. For these firms, see J. M. Price, *France and the Chesapeake,* 2 vols. (Ann Arbor, Mich., 1973), I, 620–648. Additional accounts of these firms can be found in NLS, Acc. 4796, Fettercairn Papers, boxes 200, 201, 212, 215. In box 201, Forbes gives the capital of the London house as £8,688.9.7 on 1 Jan. 1775 and the Edinburgh house as £6,211.8.4. This was perhaps before a distribution of profits. For Ayloffe, see PRO, Prob.3/21/58.

16. See *The New Statistical Account of Scotland,* 15 vols. (Edinburgh and London, 1845), VI, 230–231; confirmed by descriptions of individual firms in compensation claims in PRO, T.79 and A.O.13. For Cochrane's interests, see SRO, R.D.2/222(i), pp. 313–319.

17. See appendix B. When three or more quotations were available on a firm, only the first and last were used here. In addition, cf. Devine, *Tobacco Lords,* 75–76.

18. Mitchell Library, Glasgow, Papers of Daniel Campbell of Shawfield, no. 587.

19. See appendix A for the calculation of these "advances."

20. Contract (1754) in SRA, Glasgow Burgh Court Register of

Deeds, B10/15, no. 6653; 1761 arbitration in Glasgow Commissary Court Register of Deeds, CC 9/16/53, SRO.

21. PRO, T.79/11; and see appendix B.

22. PRO, T.79/25; SRO, CC 9/16/75; Devine, *Tobacco Lords,* 75.

23. PRO, T.79/22, 33(10).

24. PRO, T.79/1, fols. 275, 287; SRA, B10/15, no. 7606; SRO, R.D.3/309, pp. 58–81; Signet Library, Session Papers, 162/23(67–75). For this firm, see J. M. Price, "The Rise of Glasgow in the Chesapeake Tobacco Trade, 1707–1775," *William and Mary Quarterly,* 3d ser., 11 (1954), 192–197; J. H. Soltow, "Scottish Traders to Virginia," *Economic History Review,* 2d ser., 12 (1959), 83–98.

25. *Autobiography of the Rev. Dr. Alexander Carlyle, Minister of Inveresk* (Edinburgh and London, 1860), 73.

26. [Robert Reid et al.], *Glasgow Past and Present,* new ed., 3 vols. (Glasgow, 1884), I, 461; George Stewart, *Curiosities of Glasgow Citizenship as Exhibited Chiefly in the Business Careers of Its Old Commercial Aristocracy* (Glasgow, 1881), 215–217.

27. PRO, T.79/26. The firm also had branches in northern Virginia, using the style Neil Jamieson & Co. in Norfolk and Falmouth (Rappahannock), but that of Glassford, Gordon, Monteath & Co. in Cabin Point (James River), Petersburg (Appomatox), and Fredericksburg (Rappahannock).

28. LC, Neil Jamieson MSS XIV, fol. 3113, Jamieson to James Glassford, 27 June 1771. John Glassford was also the principal partner (with James Gordon, Thomas Campbell, and John Ingram) in a firm formed in 1764 with a capital of £10,000 to trade to Patuxent River, Md. This firm may have been subsequently merged with Glassford's larger firm trading to Potomac River. SRA, TD 219/9/2(1).

29. The only other indications of capitalization above £30,000 date from 1775–76: Donald, Scott & Co. (£38,226) and James & Robert Donald & Co. (£65,000). PRO, T.79/15, 18.

30. Aubrey C. Land, "Economic Behavior in a Planting Society: The Eighteenth Century Chesapeake," *Journal of Southern History,* 33 (1967), 469–485, and "Economic Base and Social Structure: The Northern Chesapeake in the Eighteenth Century," *Journal of Economic History,* 25 (1965), 639–654, esp. 639–640. In 1754, Dr. Charles Carroll of Annapolis estimated his and his son's estate at

not less than £15,000 sterling. "Extracts from Account and Letter Books of Dr. Charles Carroll of Annapolis," *Maryland Historical Magazine,* 27 (1932), 218. Henrietta Dorsey, daughter of the Maryland lawyer Edward Dorsey, allegedly left an estate of £40,000 in 1766. New York Historical Society, Wm. Lux letterbook, Lux to W. Molleson, 3 Nov. 1766. When the Hon. Philip Ludwell died ca. 1769, his estate (divided between his two daughters) was worth £24,964 sterling. VaHS, Lee (Ludwell) Papers: Green Springs Estate Papers. Charles Carroll informed his son Charles Carroll (of Carrollton) in 1764 that he considered himself worth £88,380, including, among other things, land (£44,000), slaves (£8,550), a share in an ironworks (£10,000), and loans out on interest (£24,230). MdHS, Horsey (Lee) Deposit, folder 17 (old no. P/1307). He admitted that his land estimates might be considered slightly high.

31. Henry Hamilton, *An Economic History of Scotland in the Eighteenth Century* (Oxford, 1963), 193–200.

32. These included the Greenock Sugar House (£7,027 in 1772); Easter Sugar House (£14,838 in 1742); Wester Sugar House (£9,000 in 1735 and £8,081 in 1740); the Glasgow Tanworks (£8,000 in 1738); and the New Glasgow Tanworks (£12,000 in 1758). Cf. SRA, B10/15, nos. 5042, 6124, 6268, 6871.

33. SRA, B10/15, no. 7147, Contract of copartnery (16 Apr. 1765) of McCall, Finlays & Scott, merchants in Glasgow, engaged "in buying, manufacturing & disposing of goods." Two of the partners, James McCall and Robert Scott, had other interests in the Chesapeake trade. For the partnership of Fultons, Finlay, Ure & Co., printers, see ibid., no. 7717. James Finlay was a partner in both companies. The capital of the Printfield Manufactory at Pollockshaws was £8,400 in 1759. SRO, CC9/7/63, pp. 380–382 (copy in SRA, TD 60).

34. Edward Hughes, *North Country Life in the Eighteenth Century,* vol. II, *Cumberland and Westmorland* (London, 1965), 29–30.

35. Lancashire RO, DDX/632/1. On this firm, see John W. Tyler, "Foster Cunliffe and Sons: Liverpool Merchants in the Maryland Tobacco Trade, 1738–1765," *Maryland Historical Magazine,* 73 (1978), 246–279.

36. Liverpool RO, 920 Tar, 2/1-17, 2/18/2, 2/19/1-3, 2/20/1-2, 2/21A, B. Tarleton's eldest son, Thomas (1753–1820), removed to

Bolesworth Castle, Cheshire, ca. 1790. Another son was Sir Banastre Tarleton.

37. Bristol AO, Harford Family Papers, bdls. VIII/1a (personal ledger of E. Harford, Jr.), VII/2a (ledger C), and VIII/9 (estate papers, 1806). Ledger B (1768–1779) is missing. During the last two decades or so of his life, Edward Harford, Jr., was a banker with wide industrial and other investment interests but no longer a merchant trading abroad. A century before, John Love, a Chesapeake merchant of Bristol, left personal assets of £9,944 in 1697, but his *net* estate may have been less. PRO, Prob.4/1801.

38. Greater London RO (former Middlesex section), acc. 1017 (Eliot MSS), nos. 905, 932.

39. Library of University College, Cork, MSS 31, 31A, ledger and journal of Samuel Hoare (1716–1796), with photocopy in National Library of Ireland, Dublin. For the family, see L. G. Pine, *The New Extinct Peerage, 1884–1971* (Baltimore, Md., 1973), 264–266. For the business activities of the firm, see Marten G. Buist, *At Spes Non Fracta: Hope & Co., 1770–1815: Merchant Bankers and Diplomats at Work* (The Hague, 1974), esp. 16, 21, 39; Price, *France and the Chesapeake*, 625, 630, 1048; L. M. Cullen, *Anglo-Irish Trade, 1660–1800* (Manchester, 1968), 165–167, 187, 190–191, 208; Lucy S. Sutherland, *A London Merchant, 1695–1774* (London, 1933, 1962), 138–139. For an even more impressive example of slow but steady capital accumulation in the seventeenth century by the woolendraper-merchant Thomas Cullum, see Alan Simpson, *The Wealth of the Gentry, 1540–1660: East Anglian Studies* (Cambridge and Chicago, 1961), ch. 3. For a similar but shorter pattern of accumulation in the estate of Charles Blunt, London financier, see Philip E. Mirowski, "The Birth of the Business Cycle" (Ph.D. diss., University of Michigan, 1979), 535.

40. It is not possible to be entirely certain about the capital of the firm since Samuel Hoare did not clearly distinguish, in his capital account with the firm, between his "stock" (or partnership share) in the firm and his "surplus stock" left in the firm at interest—and one cannot be sure that his partners left their "surplus stock" in the firm in the same proportions. If we assume they did, we get a capitalization (including surplus) for Gurnell, Hoare, Harman & Co. of £63,000 at the end of the partnership of 1760–1767, and a capitalization of £78,750 at the beginning and

£100,000 at the end of the partnership of 1767–1774. In 1774, Hoare appears to have retired from the firm, lending his sons the sums needed to buy out his share, but the account is not entirely clear or complete. University College, Cork, MSS 31, 31A.

41. Exeter RO, Kennaway Collection, 58/9/5/1.

42. The journal of another Exeter merchant exporting cloth to Italy, Samuel Milford (Exeter RO, 71/8), shows "Stock in Trade" rising from £2,174 on 19 Dec. 1761 to £2,659 on 31 Dec. 1763. Growth, needless to say, was not automatic. Another Exeter merchant, Thomas Jeffery, received £4,000 from his father in 1689 as a marriage portion, and an additional £1,600 with his first wife and £3,000 with his second, but his net worth in 1704 was only £8,704. Exeter RO, 61/6/1.

43. R. G. Wilson, *Gentlemen Merchants: The Merchant Community in Leeds, 1700–1830* (Manchester and New York, 1971), 32–33, 64–67, 83–84.

44. BL, Add. MS 45,022, fols. 34–54 (notes by R. P. Stearns); Add. MS 44,999; and dossier on Smith, Son & Russell in PRO, T.79/17.

45. Norfolk and Norwich RO, Gurney Papers, RQG 485–487, 496–497, 505–506. The personal estate of John Gurney increased much more rapidly than the capitalization of his firm. When he started in business with his father, Joseph, in 1741, he was worth £4,000: £1,000 of his own, £1,000 given to him by his father, and £2,000 from his wife's dowry. By 1748 he was worth £11,100, and when his father died in 1750, he inherited about £2,700 in personalty and £2,000 in realty. When he himself died in 1770, John Gurney was worth at least £81,200. Ibid., RQG 298, 300, and 302.

46. The capitalizations of other mercantile firms noted usually fall into this same range (£5,000–£20,000) before 1776. Henry Phill, a London Eastland merchant, had a net worth in his annual accounts that rose from £8,445 in 1698 to £13,431 in 1706 (PRO, C.111/127); Blackwell & Jacob, Bristol wine merchants, were capitalized at £10,890 in their partnership agreement of 1701 (PRO, C.105/29). Ball & Harford, Bristol, had a capital of £5,000, 1721–1723, for the linen trade (Bristol AO, Mark Harford ledger A); Quinn & Roche, London merchants trading to Spain, Holland, and Ireland, started with a capital of £6,000 in 1752 (PRO, E.112/1596/731); while John Pardoe & Co., wine merchants of London

and Oporto (Wells & Co.), put their capital at £18,000 in 1763 (PRO, C.105/38[ii], bdle. 41).

47. The Glasgow capital per hogshead imported has been calculated by dividing the capitals for 1772–1775 shown in appendix B by the number of hogsheads imported by the same firms there shown in: (1773) James Cleland, *The Rise and Progress of the City of Glasgow* (Glasgow, 1820), 90; (1774) James Pagan, *Sketch of the History of Glasgow* (Glasgow, 1847), 80–81; (1775) Northampton RO, Fitzwilliam-Burke MSS, A.xxv.74. During 1771–1775, *British* imports averaged £1.1 million p.a. from Virginia and Maryland and £5 million p.a. from the whole America–West Indies–Africa area. B. R. Mitchell and P. Deane, *Abstract of British Historical Statistics* (Cambridge, 1962), 310; *Historical Statistics of the United States* (1976), II, 1176–78 (correcting headings in Scottish tables).

48. On freight rates, see J. M. Hemphill II, "Freight Rates in the Maryland Tobacco Trade, 1707–1762," *Maryland Historical Magazine*, 54 (1959), 36–58, 153–187.

49. Cf. J. M. Price, "A Note on the Value of Colonial Exports of Shipping," *Journal of Economic History*, 26 (1976), 704–724; Ralph Davis, *The Rise of the English Shipping Industry in the Seventeenth and Eighteenth Centuries* (London, 1962), 267–299, 357–361.

50. There are numerous references to such chartering in the correspondence of London Maryland merchants, including James Russell and Joshua Johnson. Cf. Price, "One Family's Empire," 178, 189; idem, "Joshua Johnson in London, 1771–1775," in Anne Whiteman et al., eds., *Statesmen, Scholars and Merchants* (Oxford, 1973), 169, 175.

51. Davis, *English Shipping Industry*, 369–372.

52. PRO, C.217/86/1–3.

53. Cf. Davis, *English Shipping Industry*, 100.

54. Price, *France and the Chesapeake*, I, 597.

55. PRO, E.144/24 and 27, King v. How.

4 BORROWING ON BOND

1. Colonial Williamsburg Foundation, Norton MSS, John Norton to J. H. Norton, 4 Sept. 1773.

2. Jacob M. Price, ed., *Joshua Johnson's Letterbook, 1771–1774: Letters from a Merchant in London to His Partners in Maryland*, London Record Society, XV (London, 1979), no. 63a, to firm, 6 Feb. 1773.

The same letter mentions that James Russell also received unspecified big loans then.

3. Jack P. Greene, ed., *The Diary of Colonel Landon Carter of Sabine Hall, 1752–1778*, 2 vols. (Charlottesville, Va., 1965), II, 722–723.

4. PRO, Prob.5/1560 (Bowles), 1761 (Hall); C.111/127(1), Ledger and Journal of Henry Phill, Baltic merchant of London; E.112/1596/706 (London, Hilary Term, 6 Geo. III), Taylor v. Leybourne; D. C. Coleman, *Sir John Banks, Baronet and Businessman* (Oxford, 1973), 37–40, 56, 64, 84. See BL, Printed Books Dept., 515.1.15(106–112) for a group of printed cases in appeals to the House of Lords regarding the estate of H. Morice, esp. no. 106.

5. PRO, Prob.3/24/61 (Whitehead); Prob.5/418 (Turner); Prob.5/620 (Cole). For other examples of estates heavily invested in bonds, see PRO, C.107/43 (going back to 1635), and Berkshire RO, D/EM B18, Charles and Joseph Hatt papers. For a country estate of £6,103 with about 25 percent in bonds, see PRO, Prob.3/21/203 (inventory of J. Duppa).

6. Norfolk and Norwich RO, Gurney Papers, RQG 542.

7. Bristol AO, MS 08841(2)a-c, (3)a-e, (4)a-m, (5)a-g. One customs bond was countersigned by Sydenham Shipway, another linendraper, and another by Samuel Dykes, upholder, executor of John's brother, Walter King.

8. Bristol AO, MS 08841(1) a.1–2, b.1–5.

9. Ibid., MS 08841(6) b.1–4, 7–8. Mixed in with the bonds are counterbonds safeguarding those who countersigned King's bonds as sureties. See, e.g., ibid., b.5, 9–11. Dates before September 1752 used in this study are those of the Julian or old-style calendar; however, when such a date falls between 1 January and 24 March (inclusive), the year is shown in both old and new styles, as in February 1733/4.

10. Cf. A. H. John, "Insurance Investment and the London Money Market in the 18th Century," *Economica*, n.s., 20 (May 1953), 147–149, 151, 155; P. G. M. Dickson, *The Sun Insurance Office, 1710–1960* (London, 1960), 240–245; Barry Supple, *The Royal Exchange Assurance: A History of British Insurance, 1720–1970* (Cambridge, 1970), 73–75.

11. Bristol AO, MS 08841(6)b.6, 11-5.

12. Ibid., (7)a.1–2, b.1–3, c–e, f.1–2, h.

13. Ibid., (6)a.1-17. Other women lenders were Elizabeth Bush (£20), Elizabeth Egleston (£50), Mrs. Rachel Griffeth (£80), Susan

Harmer (£100), Mrs. Elizabeth Moxon (£131.4.0), and Mrs. Ann Willoughby (£150); other men were Benjamin Beach, tailor (£200), Samuel Pill (£75), Edward Smith (£100), John Stephen (£46), William Temple (£100), and King's son John King (a £6.5.0 legacy).

14. Bristol AO, Mark Harford Ledger A, fols. 15-6, 18-9. Some, of course, preferred to borrow from their own families. The wealthy Quaker merchant of London, Samuel Hoare, borrowed almost exclusively from his own and his wife's family. University College, Cork, MS 31, 31A, S. Hoare ledger and journal.

15. Liverpool RO, 920 Tar 2/1.

16. Ibid., 920 Tar 2/6.

17. In addition to loans to individuals, his accounts from 1769 to 1772 show £3,000–£4,500 invested in Corporation of Liverpool bonds. His accounts for 1772 show investments in the turnpike roads to Prescott (£700–£1,000) and Ormskirk (£200). Ibid., 920 Tar 2/18/2, 2/19/1, 2/20/1, 2/21A,B.

18. Ibid., 920 Tar 2/19/3.

19. B. L. Anderson, "The Attorney and the Early Capital Market in Lancashire," in J. R. Harris, ed., *Liverpool and Merseyside: Essays in the Economic and Social History of the Port and Its Hinterland* (London, 1969), 56–66, 68, 70 (quotation). For similar intermediary activities by lawyers in Bristol and Glasgow, see Bristol AO, AC/WO3(1), account book of Henry Woolnough, 1727–1736; and SRA T-MJ 1, 3, ledgers of T. & A. Grahame.

20. Cumbria RO, Carlisle, Lonsdale Papers, 1st dep., J. Spedding's letterbook (1742–1745), Spedding to Lowther, 16, 23 Jan. 1742/3 (nos. 69, 72); J. M. Price, *France and the Chesapeake,* 2 vols. (Ann Arbor, Mich., 1973), I, 597.

21. Cumbria RO, Carlisle, Lonsdale Papers, 5th dep., box D, no. 7, Sir James Lowther's letterbook (1769), Lowther to Wordsworth, 25 Apr. 1769.

22. R. G. Wilson, *Gentlemen Merchants: The Merchant Community in Leeds, 1700–1830* (Manchester and New York, 1971), 153–154. Accepting deposits as a courtesy was, however, the practice of several London breweries, which usually paid 5 percent on such privileged deposits from friends, relations, and senior employees of the proprietors, and 4 percent on deposits from attached publicans, petty suppliers, and savings "clubs" at some public houses. Nothing is reported about the use of bonds or promissory notes to

secure even the largest such deposits. Peter Mathias, *The Brewing Industry in England, 1700–1830* (Cambridge, 1959), 267, 277–281, 291–293.

23. The Thomas Jeffery ledger (Exeter RO, 61/6/1), pp. 81–83, shows that his father, Andrew (1637–1713), in his last years as a retired merchant had over £4,000 lent to others, including merchants, on bond (or mortgage in some cases). On a loose sheet is a bond of 1721 for £2,104.9.0 from William Jeffery, merchant of Exeter, to his half-brother Thomas, then retired. When Thomas's daughter Margaret married Edmund Cock, Jr., in 1710, Thomas paid her dowry of £3,500 in bonds and notes, from seventeen persons, of from £50 to £650 each. The journal of Samuel Milford, merchant of Exeter, 1760–1774 (Exeter RO, 71/8), indicates long-term borrowing of £1,500 at 4 percent from "father Milford" and £800–£1,000 also at 4 percent from "mother" Ann Moor. The Kennaway accounts (Exeter RO, 58/9) give few details before the 1780s, but in 1783–1793 we find evidence of bonded debt by the Kennaways to Sir Robert Falk, Bart. (£2,000), Richard Kennaway (£2,000), R. Lenton (£1,500), R. Troyte of Bustards (£1,400), Rev. A. Tozer (£1,200), the executors of T. Turner (£1,000), and the executors of S. Churchill (£600).

24. BL, Add. MS 45,022, fol. 54; Add. MS 44,998, fols. 5, 12-4, 21.

25. The papers of Richard Oswald of Auchincruive contain letters of January 1770 from Andrew Cochrane requesting a loan on bond of up to £2,000 for William Cuninghame & Co., and from Alexander Speirs requesting one of up to £4,000 for his Virginia and Maryland houses. It is not clear if these requests were satisfied. However, Oswald had lent Speirs £1,200 on bond in 1764, a debt still outstanding in 1770—along with other bonded loans of £1,000 to Craig, Stark & Miller and £2,000 to Cochrane & Co. (later, Cuninghames). Other letters show Oswald lending substantial sums to his nephews, George and Alexander Oswald of Glasgow: £1,000, £1,500, £2,000 at a time to their Virginia concern, and £2,000 to their "Osnaburgh Linen Company" and £1,000 to "Sandy" Brown, its manager. In addition, he appears to have lent £1,000–£1,500 to W. Laird and J. Stevenson to buy a share in James McCall's Virginia concern. Richard Oswald was a Scot who made a fortune in London in privateering during the Seven Years' War and in the slave trade and then returned to Scotland as a landed proprietor. See NLS, Oswald MSS, fols. 350–50v; and mun-

iments of Major Richard Oswald, letters from J. Stevenson (4 Jan. 1767), W. Laird (28 Jan. 1767), A. Speirs (3 Jan. 1770), G. Oswald (5 Jan., 15 Oct. 1770, 6 Aug. 1772, 1 Sept. 1773), A. Oswald (24 July, 16 Aug. 1771), and Michael Herries (4 Jan. 1768). Later in the century, larger bonds may have been more common. The estate of James Somervell of Hamilton Farm, a semiretired Glasgow merchant, contained at least £13,000 lent on bond to various local concerns in units of £1,000–£2,000 (31 May 1791). SRA, T-MJ 108, p. 13.

26. Based on examination of scores of bonds and inventories in Glasgow Burgh Court and Commissary Court Registers of Deeds (SRA and SRO). For examples, see n. 31.

27. SRA, B10/15, no. 8045.

28. Based on examination of Glasgow bonds and discharges, 1720s–1770s, particularly in SRA, Burgh Court Register of Deeds (B10/15). For some intimation of the increasing scale of such lending, compare the bonded debt of Robert Robertson, a small Virginia merchant of 1740, described in T. M. Devine, *Tobacco Lords: A Study of the Tobacco Merchants of Glasgow and Their Trading Activities* (Edinburgh, 1975), 95, with that of Buchanan, Hastie & Co. (failed 1777), ibid., 94, and SRO, C.S.230 Sequestrations, B.1/1. The SRO source does not distinguish bonded from other debt, but sums lent by women, doctors, and officers were presumably lent on bond. Robert Dinwiddie, ex-governor of Virginia, lent £1,000 at 4.75 percent to Archibald Ingram & Co. (1758) through his brother, Provost Lawrence Dinwiddie of Glasgow. SRA, TD 132/68. For an example of an army officer lending £1,800 to Glasgow merchants on bond, see 1760 inventory of Capt. Walter Graham in SRO, CC9/7/63, no. 35, pp. 513–529. On the diverse sources of bonded and other credit available, see also T. M. Devine, "Sources of Capital for the Glasgow Tobacco Trade, c. 1740–1780," *Business History*, 16 (1974) 113–129, esp. tables II–IV.

29. SRA, T-MJ 1, pp. 297, 308; T-MJ 3, p. 93. About 1785–1791, Findlay, Hopkirk & Co. borrowed £1,000 on bond from the earl of Stair. SRO, C.S.96/2240.

30. SRA, B10/15, no. 6022. Most of the bonds and accepted bills of exchange were expressed in Scots *merks* and have been converted into sterling at 18 to 1. The same pattern of diversified lending to a variety of merchants can be found in the "dispositions" of retired merchants (see n. 31).

31. SRO, CC9/7/64, pp. 337-343. Similar clusters of bonds can be found in the estate inventories of other retired Glasgow merchants. Bigger than most was the £13,422 personal estate of James Spreull (d. 1769), including twenty-nine bonds (all from local merchants) totaling £12,050 for a quite high average of £446.6.0. SRO, CC9/7/67, pp. 202-212. Earlier, in 1756, Provost Peter Murdoch, a semiretired merchant, left specific bequests of £2,050 in thirteen bonds (from £50 to £400 each) averaging £157.14.0. SRA, B10/15, no. 7144.

32. Based on examination of Orphans' Court inventories of 1724 and later, in boxes 49-56, London Corporation RO. For an examination of this same material in the generation preceding the founding of the Bank of England in 1694, see articles by R. Grassby cited in ch. 1, n. 2.

33. A list of £40,192 of "Cash borrowed by Glasgow Tanwork Company on Bonds and Bills" in 1765 shows £1,742 obtained at 4.5 percent, £830 at 4.75 percent, and £37,620 (93 percent) at 5 percent. [R. Reid et al.], *Glasgow Past and Present*, new ed., 3 vols. (Glasgow, 1884), I, 467-469.

34. P. G. M. Dickson, *The Financial Revolution in England* (London, 1967), 256, 276, 294, 297, 301-302.

35. Dickson (*Financial Revolution*, 251-253) discusses this possibility but discounts it. Yet the inventory of Sir Peter Delmé of London shows that, in addition to a personal estate of over £200,000, "the Testator was at the time of his decease poss[ess]ed of several publick Stocks and other Securities which were no part of his Estate but stood in his Name only in Trust for several Persons which have been disposed of according to their respective Orders," totaling £199,720 in valued company and government stock, plus thirty-five unvalued exchequer annuities, ten unvalued shares in the London Assurance, and a £4,000 mortgage. London Corporation RO, Orphans' Court Inventories, box 50. Richard Nicholls, a London goldsmith, in 1722 left £13,484 worth of Bank and South Sea stock in his name but belonging to others. Ibid., box 55. Of another great operator, it was reported in a law suit that in the summer of 1720, "Sir Justus Beck Bought and Sold great Quantities of [Royal Exchange Assurance shares], on many different Accounts, and in his own Name, tho' in Trust for others." *John Martin de Ron* [et al.], *Appellants . . . Gerard Vaneck . . . Respondent . . . the Case of the Said De Ron's* ([London], 1731), in BL (Printed

Books), 515.1.15(14). The balance books of Martins Bank (Barclays Bank Ltd.) reveal that it held shares and bonds in its name for others, while the correspondence of Sir William Forbes reveals that similar paper owned by his Edinburgh bank was left in the control of the house's London correspondents. NLS, Fettercairn Papers (acc. 4796), box 199, Wickenden & Co. to Forbes & Co., 19 Nov. 1776, and Forbes & Co. to Wickenden & Co., 10 Dec. 1776. Several minor cases could also be cited of persons in America buying company and government stock through merchants in London. Cf. also John, "Insurance Investment."

36. See note 32.

37. B. L. Anderson, "Provincial Aspects of the Financial Revolution of the Eighteenth Century," *Business History,* 11 (1969), 11–22 (esp. 21). See also "Money and the Structure of Credit in the Eighteenth Century," ibid., 12 (1970), 85–101.

38. See John, "Insurance Investment," 137–158 (esp. 149–150, 155–156); T. S. Ashton, *Economic Fluctuations in England, 1700–1800* (Oxford, 1959), 85–88; D. M. Joslin, "London Bankers in Wartime, 1739–84," in L. S. Pressnell, ed., *Studies in the Industrial Revolution* (London, 1960), 165–172; L. S. Pressnell, "The Rate of Interest in the Eighteenth Century," ibid., 187–214 (esp. 178–180).

39. This treatment must be quite impressionistic as the mortgage market in Scotland remains to be studied.

40. William Mure of Caldwell, ed., *Selections from the Family Papers Preserved at Caldwell,* Maitland Club (Glasgow, 1854), II, pt. 1, 209–220; LC, Neil Jamieson MSS, fols. 68–69, John Glassford to Neil Jamieson, Glasgow, 16 July 1761.

41. PRO, T.79/11.

42. SRA, B10/15, no. 7606.

43. PRO, T.79/26.

44. See, e.g., John McCall & Co., in SRA, B10/15, no. 8123. No. 8046 shows that Bogle, Somervell & Co., with a capital of £6,500, had £7,116 borrowed on bond in 1776.

45. *The New Statistical Account of Scotland,* 15 vols. (Edinburgh and London, 1845), VI, 230–231.

46. Price, *Joshua Johnson's Letterbook,* no. 88, Johnson to firm, 2 July 1773.

47. MdHS, Horsey Deposit, no. 566/155, Uriah Forrest to T. S. Lee, 20 June 1785.

48. See PRO, E.190/1209/2, for Bristol tobacco imports, 1733; Price, *Joshua Johnson's Letterbook*, 158–159, and Northampton RO, Fitzwilliam (Burke) MSS, A.xxv.74, for London and Glasgow imports, 1775. On the duties and bonds, see Jacob M. Price, "The Tobacco Trade and the Treasury" (Ph.D. diss., Harvard University, 1954), chs. 1, 10 (esp. pp. 2, 810–811); and Samuel M. Rosenblatt, "The Significance of Credit in the Tobacco Consignment Trade: A Study of John Norton & Sons, 1768–1775," *William and Mary Quarterly*, 3d ser., 19 (1962), 389–394. Rosenblatt shows Norton's sales in 1775 as 1,456 hogsheads. This most likely includes some tobacco imported in previous years or perhaps entered in other merchants' names.

5 BORROWING FROM BANKS

1. Bank of England Secretary's Office, Bank Court Minutes D, 99 (30 Oct. 1701). Later, the younger Micajah Perry received extraordinary discount facilities of £3,500 to £8,000 on three occasions in 1721–1723. Ibid., Minutes, I, 16, 152, 226.

2. The Bank of England Drawing Office account (Bank RO, Roehampton) of the Virginia merchant Humphrey Bell, 1723–1745 (Ledgers 53–158), shows regular payments to a wide circle of other Virginia merchants of London, suggesting that he was paying them for bills drawn on him. It is uncertain whether the Bank discounted bills on him or for him.

3. VaHS, Lee Papers, W. Lee to R. H. Lee, 4 Mar. 1773; Jacob M. Price, ed., *Joshua Johnson's Letterbook, 1771–1774: Letters from a Merchant in London to His Partners in Maryland*, London Record Society, XV (London, 1979), no. 45, Johnson to firm, 17 July 1772.

4. S. G. Checkland, *Scottish Banking: A History* (Glasgow, 1975), 69, 81–83. A notarial document of 1758 refers to the partnership of Peter Murdoch [Sr.] and his sons, Peter [Jr.] and John, carrying on a "Banking Business" in 1734. SRA, B10/15, no. 7145. For Robertson, see B10/15, no. 5357.

5. Bank of Scotland, Court of Directors Minute Book, III pt. 2, 121, 237, 297.

6. Ibid., IV, 10, 12, 14, 16, 33. On this bank, cf. Checkland, *Scottish Banking*, 23–48.

7. The career of William Alexander is discussed in J. M. Price, *France and the Chesapeake*, 2 vols. (Ann Arbor, Mich., 1973), I, 605–617.

8. Royal Bank of Scotland, Court of Directors Minutes, V, 229–235. The first Glasgow "open cash account" was granted Sept. 20, 1728, to Alexander's connection, Peter Murdoch [Sr.] for £2,000, with sureties Peter Murdoch [Jr.], Zacharias Murdoch, and Andrew Cochrane. Ibid., I, 167. Of the twenty-four accounts cited, only three were for £1,000, one for £1,500 (John Murdoch), and one for £2,000 (Peter and John Murdoch). The remaining nineteen were for from £200 to £600. On this bank, cf. Checkland, *Scottish Banking*, 57–66, 83–84.

9. Bank of Scotland, Court of Directors Minute Books, IV, 6–9. Approximately thirty-eight Glasgow accounts were authorized between 1729 and 1749.

10. Liverpool RO, 920 TAR 2/4, 6, 7.

11. Norfolk and Norwich RO, Gurney Papers, RQG 496.

12. Friends House Library, Euston, Gurney Papers 2/510B and 511, two printed notices of 1784 about credit terms for Gurney & Bland's yarn sales.

13. L. S. Pressnell, *Country Banking in the Industrial Revolution* (Oxford, 1956).

14. For the partners, see [Robert Reid et al.], *Glasgow Past and Present*, new ed., 3 vols. (Glasgow, 1884), I, 470–486. A fourth bank, the Merchant Banking Company of Glasgow, was formed in 1769. Its partners were smaller merchants and traders in the town, but no "tobacco lords." Cf. Checkland, *Scottish Banking*, 97–103.

15. John Hughes, *Liverpool Banks & Bankers, 1760–1837* (Liverpool, 1906), 56, 84, 91–105, 118, 127–129, 141–143. Staniforth continued the mercantile business of the Chesapeake trader Charles Goore, who started as a ship captain for the Cunliffes, the greatest Liverpool traders to the Chesapeake at mid-century. John Tarleton's son Thomas banked with both the Heywood and Clay (Gregson's) banks.

16. Charles Henry Cave, *A History of Banking in Bristol from 1750 to 1899* (Bristol, 1899), 9–12.

17. Only three Virginia or Maryland merchant firms had drawing accounts at the Bank of England in 1750–1775: Edward Athawes, Anthony Bacon, and Thomas & Daniel Mildred. The Mildreds also banked with their fellow Quaker, Freame.

18. F. G. Hilton Price, *A Handbook of London Bankers* (London, 1876), 160–166; enlarged ed. (1890–91), 187–195.

19. Index and ledger for the year 1 Oct. 1774–30 Sept. 1775 at

archives of National Westminster Bank Ltd. Peter Martin deposited Chesapeake-trade bills of exchange in his account.

20. Archives of the former Glyn, Mills & Co., Hallifax, Mills Christmas book (1774); Curries "Banking Stock Book," 1774. Hallifax, Mills customers did include Langkopf, Molling & Rasch, buyers of tobacco and suppliers of German linens to the Chesapeake trade.

21. Also at archives of National Westminster Bank Ltd.

22. On Grote, see London directories; Harriet Lewin Grote, *The Personal Life of George Grote*, 2d ed. (London, 1873), 1–3, 9; M. L. Clarke, *George Grote: A Biography* (London, 1962), 1–4, 186.

23. MdHR, Joshua Johnson's London journal (Private Accounts no. 1514), p. 104.

24. Martins Bank archives (now part of Barclays Bank Ltd.), Lombard St., London, discount book, annual balances, and ledger 1.

25. P. W. Matthews and A. W. Tuke, *History of Barclays Bank Limited* (London, 1926), 32–38. For a reference to Thomas Gould and John Freame in the Virginia trade, see PRO, T.1/112/23. On Barclays' American connections, see Price, *Joshua Johnson's Letterbook*, no. 41b to partners, 22 June 1772; LC, R. Pleasants letterbook, to Farell & Jones, and to D. & J. Barclay, 10 Jan. 1774. For Gould's failure, see PRO, Ind. 22640 (B.4/7), p. 212.

26. The following section is based on the annual balance and discount books of the Freame-Barclay bank, 1748–1799, at the head office, Barclays Bank Ltd., London.

27. Price, *Joshua Johnson's Letterbook*, no. 157, Johnson to firm, 4 Aug. 1774.

28. See note 32; R. S. Sayers, *Lloyds Bank in the History of English Banking* (Oxford, 1957), 5–17; Hilton Price, *London Bankers* (1890–91), 13–14, 113. John Bland of Lombard Street, banker and goldsmith, failed in 1720 but was able to resume business by 1728. PRO, Ind. 22636 (B.4/3), pp. 141, 157.

29. The banking firms of Denne & Co. (1774), Mildred & Co. (1778), and Coutts & Co. had historic but not current connections with the tobacco trade.

30. Walpole, Clarke & Bourne; Robert Herries & Co.; Bland, Barnett & Hoare.

31. Dorrien, Rucker & Carleton; Prescotts, Grote, Culverden & Hollingworth; Smith, Bevan & Bening (Barclays); Smith, Payne &

Smith. Outside London, wholesale linendrapers were also conspicuous in banking, e.g., William Clarke & Sons of Liverpool, and the Bath Old Bank.

32. MdHR, J. Johnson's London journal (Private Accounts nos. 1513–15); Price, *Joshua Johnson's Letterbook*, no. 6a, Johnson to firm, 26 July 1771.

33. Charles W. Barclay et al., *A History of the Barclay Family*, 3 vols. (London, 1924–1934), III, 249–250; Sayers, *Lloyds Bank*, 10.

34. For example, the "Banking Stock Book" of Curries Bank (at the former Glyn, Mills & Co., London) shows that partners owed the firm £21,750 against nominal paid-in capital of £30,000. One of them, John Mason, a warehouseman, owed £10,000, equal to his full share of the capital.

35. Barclays Bank Ltd., annual balances, 1748–1799.

36. Martins Bank archives (Barclays Bank Ltd.), Trial Balance Book (1731–1744), Christmas Balance Book (1742–1748, 1755–1760), General Balance Book (1746–1752). Robert Surman established a bank of his own but failed in 1757. His bank continued as Walpole, Clarke & Bourne. PRO, Ind. 22646 (B.4/5), fol. 28.

37. Sayers, *Lloyds Bank*, 11.

38. Archives of the former Glyn, Mills & Company, London, Curries' "Banking Stock Book," 1774.

39. National Westminster Bank archives, Prescotts, Grote & Co.'s partnership agreements of 1776 and 1792, and Summary Book, 1780–1865.

40. National Westminster Bank archives, no. 2245, articles of partnership of 7 Apr. 1758 between Abel Smith (two-thirds) and John Payne (one-third), and indenture (March 1765) between Abel Smith and the executors of John Payne, releasing Payne's share in the bank for £5,000. Since Payne held one-third, the full capital of the bank then was valued at £15,000.

41. Ibid., no. 3981. This contract also provided that the partners were to bring in more capital as needed.

42. Ibid., no. 3980.

43. Ibid., nos. 3982, 4559 (partnership contracts of 1773 and 1788); Smiths' Nottingham Balance, 30 Dec. 1780. For a fuller account, see J. A. S. L. Leighton-Boyce, *Smiths the Bankers, 1658–1958* (London, 1958), 67–82.

44. National Westminster Bank archives, General Balance Book

of the Bristol Old Bank (Lloyd, Elton, Miller, Tyndall, Gillam & Edye), 1772–1782; Sayers, *Lloyds Bank,* 5. With changes in partners, the capital of the Bristol Old Bank fell to £24,000 in 1777–1780 and £18,000 in 1781–82.

45. On the Ship Bank see SRA, TD 161-1, Ship Bank Balance Book, 1752–1761; Checkland, *Scottish Banking,* 107; SRO, CC9/7/ 65, pp. 453–455. The figures for the Glasgow Arms Bank are estimates derived from valuations of shares at transfers, in SRO, CC9/7/62, p. 491, and CC9/7/63, pp. 5–6, 277–278, 604.

46. NLS, Fettercairn Papers (acc. 4796), boxes 200 and 201.

47. National Westminster Bank archives, Bristol Old Bank General Balance Book.

48. Martins Bank archives (Barclays Bank Ltd.), General Balance Book (1746–1752), pp. 31–32, 62.

49. Barclays Bank Ltd., Discount Book, E, fol. 22, K, fol. 43, L, fol. 33. In the year ending 25 June 1772, the firm's distribution was £5,205 or 26 percent of capital, but in the depression year ending 26 June 1773 it was only £2,736 or 13.7 percent. Cf. also Sayers, *Lloyds Bank,* 10.

50. National Westminster Bank archives, Prescotts, Grote & Co. Summary Book (1780–1865).

51. Ibid.

52. Ibid.; Martins Bank archives as given in note 36.

53. Barclays Bank Ltd., annual balances, 1748–1799.

54. See note 38.

55. National Westminster Bank archives, Abel Smith & Co. (Nottingham) balance, 30 Dec. 1780; Leighton-Boyce, *Smiths the Bankers,* 315.

56. See note 47; Sayers, *Lloyds Bank,* 10; Sir John Clapham, *The Bank of England,* 2 vols. (Cambridge, 1944), I, 169, 205.

57. Rondo Cameron et al., *Banking in the Early Stages of Industrialization* (New York, 1967), 66.

58. NLS, MS 4942, fols. 156–157, J. Campbell et al. to W. Mure, Glasgow, 12 Jan. 1763; SRA, B10/15, nos. 7432, 7498; Checkland, *Scottish Banking,* 107. See also [Reid et al.], *Glasgow Past and Present,* I, 478.

59. See Ship Bank sources listed in note 45.

60. NLS, Fettercairn Papers (acc. 4796), box 201.

61. Barclays Bank Ltd., annual balances, 1748–1799.

62. Accounts cited in note 36.

63. See note 50.
64. See note 47.
65. NLS, Fettercairn Papers (acc. 4796), box 201 (1788 annual accounts); and box 199, Wickenden, Moffatt, Kensington & Co. to Forbes, Hunter & Co., 19 Nov. 1776, and latter to former, 10 Dec. 1776; Sir William Forbes of Pitsligo, *Memoirs of a Banking House*, 2d ed. (London and Edinburgh, 1860), 73, 92; for Martins' holding of shares in their own name for Samson Gideon and others, see their General Balance Book (1746–1752), pp. 26–29.
66. NLS, Fettercairn Papers (acc. 4796), box 199, Forbes, Hunter & Co.'s correspondence with Wickenden, Moffatt & Co. and with Coutts & Co., 1776–1777.
67. National Westminster Bank archives, Abel Smith's letterbook, J. Glassford to E. Payne, Dougalstoun, 20 Oct. 1772.
68. SRO, C.S.96/2025, State of Ranking, James Dunlop, 1776–77, p. 142; CC9/16/55 (registered 20 Dec. 1763).
69. Martins Bank archives (Barclays Bank Ltd.), ledger, 1770–1772.
70. VaSL, Norton Cash Book.
71. PRO, E.144/27, King v. Neale (1772). The partners were Henry Neale, William James, Alexander Fordyce, and Richard Down.
72. National Westminster Bank archives, partnership contract of 28 Nov. 1776 between George Prescott (one-tenth), George William Prescott (his eldest son, two-tenths), Andrew Grote (two-tenths), Joseph Grote (his eldest son, one-tenth), William Culverden (two-tenths), and John Hollingworth the elder (one-tenth).
73. The discount books preserved in the Barclays Bank vaults show that among the bills of exchange discounted were those of the London buying agents of the French tobacco monopoly (Herries, Walpole, Bourdieu in particular), while bills discounted for David & John Barclay (wholesale linendrapers and American merchants) included some on well-known names in the Chesapeake trade (Russell, Bogle, Gildart, Hanbury, Gale, Harford). Books E, F, K, L, and M were examined.
74. The Martins Bank 1731–1735 discount book (Barclays Bank Ltd.) shows discounting for the following Chesapeake merchants: John Hyde & Co., James Buchanan, Humphrey Bell, Silvanus Grove.
75. For the West End banks, see D. M. Joslin, "London Private

Bankers, 1720–1785," *Economic History Review*, 2d ser., 7 (1954), 167–186, and "London Bankers in Wartime, 1739–84," in *Studies in the Industrial Revolution Presented to T. S. Ashton*, ed. L. S. Pressnell (London, 1960), 156–177. The late Professor Joslin utilized the records of several West End banks (particularly Hoares, Goslings, and Childs) but only one City bank (Martins). The West End banks had little connection with merchants trading abroad and are thus of only limited interest for this study.

76. Martins Bank archives (Barclays Bank Ltd.), General Balance Book (1746–1752), and Christmas Balance Book (1755–1760). The use of the term "overdraft" in this paragraph does not imply the existence of a modern systematic overdraft institution but simply the handling of credit advances by ledger entries only (creating negative balances) rather than by bond, note, or bill. It is possible, of course, that in England such negative balances were secured by accepted bills of exchange left for collection or otherwise. Contemporary merchants commonly allowed their valued correspondents minor debit balances as a courtesy.

77. National Westminster Bank archives, Prescotts, Grote & Co. Summary Balance Book (1780–1865).

78. Leighton-Boyce, *Smiths the Bankers*, 315; National Westminster Bank archives, Abel Smith & Co., Nottingham, balance, 30 Dec. 1780; cf. also Sayers, *Lloyds Bank*, 10. Overdrafts were of comparable importance at Nottingham in 1748 and 1752.

79. See note 47.

80. SRA, TD 161-1, Ship Bank Balance Book, 1752–1761 (list at end). The £2,000 limit was granted to Alexander Houstoun & Co. and to Buchanan & Simson. Alexander Houstoun and George Buchanan were partners in the bank. Insiders were also given favorable treatment in regard to repayment. When the old partnership in the Ship Bank was wound up in 1775, Alexander Houstoun & Co. and George Oswald & Co. each owed the bank (in which Houstoun and Oswald were partners) £1,500. These debts were left outstanding but were considered security for unredeemed paper. SRO, CC 9/16/74.

81. SRA, B10/15, no. 8046; SRO, C.S.96/504, fols. 123–126. When the successor firm, Simson, Baird & Co., failed in 1772, only £1,059 was owing to the Old [Ship] Bank out of debts of £26,287. SRO, C.S.231 Sequestrations, S.1/1 (Simson, Baird & Co.).

82. London Corporation RO, Orphans' Court inventories, box 29.

83. MdHR, Private Accounts 1519, J. Johnson's London journal, 1774-75.

84. SRO, C.S.96/508.

6 COMMERCIAL CREDIT

1. BL, Add. MS 33,030, fols. 161-162. A Virgina merchant of Ayr explained, "The Virg[ini]a old debts can never be depended on till we have them in our Pockets—Those owing to my fathers old Concern which I left behind me 14 years ago [1749] are not yet settled." Muniments of Sir James Hunter Blair, Bart., James Hunter, Sr., to nephew James, Jr., Ayr, 29 Aug. 1763. For comparison with conditions in the trade to Portugal, see H. E. S. Fisher, *The Portugal Trade . . . 1700-1770* (London, 1971), 37-38, 53, 58-60, 75-76, 81-85.

2. See, e.g., MdHR, Private Accounts 1517, Wallace, Davidson & Johnson ledger B, fol. 93, account of Samuel Coldberg or Coleberg.

3. SRO, RH15/1189, Lawson & Semple ledger (Glasgow). In order to get higher prices in a difficult market and to impress the consigners in Virginia, London commission merchants selling primarily to the inland trade sometimes conceded up to six months' credit. Cf. VaHS, Lee Papers, W. Lee to R. H. Lee, 31 Dec. 1771.

4. See Jacob M. Price, "The Tobacco Trade and the Treasury" (Ph.D. diss., Harvard University, 1954), I, 17.

5. Based on buying patterns measurable in the ledgers and other records of Joshua Johnson (see note 2) and the sales book of John Norton & Son, VaSL.

6. Richard Campbell, *The London Tradesman* (London, [1747]; reprinted, 1969), 273-274, 339, 340.

7. The inventory (1676) of Richard Hunt, of the parish of St. Botolph without Aldgate, Middlesex, tobacco cutter, shows goods and debts ("most of them desperatt") totaling £437.6.10 but gives no information on the amounts he owed. PRO, Prob.4/289. The inventory (1669) of Thomas Foster, citizen and "baker" of London (actually a tobacconist), reveals insolvency, with debts owed (£57) exceeding personal property and good debts (£56.5.0). London Corporation RO, Orphans' Court inventories, box 54, no. 98. Also

insolvent was Thomas Marsham, citizen and haberdasher of London but "by trade a tobacconist," whose personal property and good debts totaled only £561 but whose obligations came to £929. Ibid., box 52, roll 10.

8. The inventory (1734) of Thomas Wagstaffe, tobacconist "by Aldgate" (nominally an ironmonger), showed a net estate of £2,860, while that (1747) of Giles Hitchman (nominally a cooper) came to £2,285. Wagstaffe was a much more important tobacconist than Hitchman, more than half (£1,428) of whose estate was represented by "Stock in the Public Funds." London Corporation RO, Orphans' Court inventories, box 51 (Wagstaffe) and box 56, no. 241 (Hitchman).

9. London Corporation RO, Orphans' Court inventories, box 42 (Francis Levett), box 50 (Sandwell), box 56, no. 234 (Spencer); Kent AO, U513/B1 (Bosworth & Griffith); *Political State of Great Britain*, 49 (1735), 203 (Matthews). When Sir John Bosworth died in 1752, the capital of Bosworth & Griffith was £10,000. PRO, Prob. 11/796 (P.C.C. 205 Bettesworth).

10. E.g., James and Robert Berrie in Lawson & Semple ledger, SRO, RH 15/1189. The Glasgow tobacco manufacturer, John Tilloch & Co., had a "capital stock" of £3,798 in 1780. SRA, B10/15, no. 8309.

11. Jacob M. Price, *France and the Chesapeake*, 2 vols. (Ann Arbor, Mich., 1973), ch. 25.

12. SRO, RH 15/1189 (Lawson & Semple ledger) esp. fol. 15. See also "Letters of Charles Carroll, Barrister," *Maryland Historical Magazine*, 32 (1937), 40; *The New Statistical Account of Scotland*, 15 vols. (Edinburgh and London, 1845), VI, 231; MdHR, Wallace, Davidson & Johnson ledgers A and B (Private Accounts, nos. 1516, 1517); and Jacob M. Price, ed., *Joshua Johnson's Letterbook, 1771–1774: Letters from a Merchant in London to His Partners in Maryland*, London Record Society, XV (London, 1979), nos. 6, 14, 17, Johnson to firm, 26 July, 17 Sept., 2 Dec. 1771. For a 15-month credit on a sale of hats for export in Glasgow, see SRO, C.S.230 B/5/8. For 15- and 18-month credits in London, see *Joshua Johnson's Letterbook*, no. 19, Johnson to firm, 4 Dec. 1771.

13. VaSL, Allason MSS, box 8, Clay & Parry to Allason, 6 May 1784.

14. Many examples appear in MdHR, Wallace, Davidson & Johnson ledgers and journals.

15. Price, "Tobacco Trade and the Treasury," II, 810–811.

16. LC, Custis letterbook, fol. 7, J. Custis to H. Bell, 1718; New York Public Library, Custis MSS, accounts of sale from Lyonel Lyde & Co., 1733–1745; VaHS, Custis MSS, accounts of sale from Hanbury & Co., 1742–1750 and later. After Custis's death, George Washington, as guardian of Custis's children, obtained similar rebates for the Custis estate in the 1760s and 1770s from Hanburys and Carys in London, plus interest on the balance left in London over what was needed to pay the duties. See later accounts of sale and also Washington's Custis estate account books, VaHS, MS 5:3 W277, 1–2. For an earlier example of a London merchant allowing a consigning planter the full customs-house discount, provided he had the necessary balance, see LC, Galloway Papers, Higginson & Bird letterbook, no. 1867 to C. Fleming, 24 Dec. 1718. See also the Jones reference in note 17. This practice was discussed at the time of the "excise affair" of 1733. Cf. *The Case of the Planters of Tobacco in Virginia . . . To Which is Added, A Vindication of the said Representation* (London, 1733), 53–56; *Considerations Relating to the Tobacco Trade at London, so far as it Relates to the Merchants Who are Factors* ([London, 1733]), 2; *A Reply to the Vindication of the Representation of the Case of the Planters of Tobacco in a Letter to Sir J[ohn] R[andolph]* (London, 1733), 42–43.

17. LC, Jones MSS, fols. 1019, 1601-02, 1864, 2025, 2513, 2670. (On at least one occasion in 1765, Jones also received sixteen months' full discount in London: fol. 2757.) The Bristol merchants gave their Virginia consignors the full 7 percent customs-house discount for half (nine months) of the eighteen months for which it was allowed. Presumably they counted on being in funds by the last nine months. See also other Bristol accounts of sale in: University of North Carolina, Chapel Hill, Southern Historical Collections, C. W. Dabney MSS, 1/9 (30 May 1758) and 1/62 (25 July 1755); Huntington Library, San Marino, Calif. Tinsley MSS, BR, box 16, August 1747. At least one Bristol merchant tried the more generous scheme of allowing the consignor the full discount for eighteen months while charging him interest for funds used to obtain the discount. This was not understood by the planter and was dropped. Circular letter from Henry Lippincott & Co., February 1775, VaSL, Allason MSS, box 7. Professor Rosenblatt (in his table) exaggerates almost fourfold the merchant's gains from the discounts by failing to deduct the cost of

the money used to obtain the discount. S. M. Rosenblatt, "The Significance of Credit in the Tobacco Consignment Trade: A Study of John Norton & Sons, 1768–1775," *William and Mary Quarterly,* 3d ser., 19 (1962), 391–394.

18. Price, *Joshua Johnson's Letterbook,* no. 31, Johnson to firm, 25 March 1772.

19. Ralph Davis, "English Foreign Trade, 1660–1700," *Economic History Review,* 2d ser., 7 (1954–1955), 164–165; idem, "English Foreign Trade, 1700–1774," ibid., 15 (1962–1963), 291–292, 302–303.

20. Julia de L. Mann, *The Cloth Industry in the West of England from 1640 to 1880* (Oxford, 1971), 63–85; E. A. L. Moir, "The Gentlemen Clothiers: A Study of the Organization of the Gloucestershire Cloth Industry, 1750–1835," in H. P. R. Finberg, ed., *Gloucestershire Studies* (Leicester, 1957), 232–239; Ephraim Lipson, *The Economic History of England,* 6th ed. (London, 1956), II, 25–31; Ray Bert Westerfield, *Middlemen in English Business, Particularly between 1660 and 1760,* Transactions of the Connecticut Academy of Arts and Sciences, 19 (New Haven, 1915), 296–304; B. E. Supple, *Commercial Crisis and Change in England, 1600–1642* (Cambridge, 1959), 40–41; William Maitland, *The History of London,* 2 vols. (London, 1756), I, 462–467. For earlier credit arrangements, see introduction by R. H. Tawney to Thomas Wilson, *A Discourse upon Usury* (London and New York, 1925), 43–49.

21. The controversial literature of 1692–1714 is interesting though tendentious. See, for example, *The Clothiers Complaint: or, Reasons for Passing the Bill against the Blackwell-Hall Factors* (London, 1692); *Reasons for Preserving the Publick Market of Blackwell-Hall* (n.p., [ca. 1696]); Dum Spiro Spero [pseud.], *An Humble Representation of the State of our Woollen Manufactures* (London, 1700); *The Clothiers Reasons for Petitioning the Commons of Great Britain . . . to Oblige all Buyers of Cloth upon Credit to Give Notes . . .* (n.p., [1714]).

22. Isaac de Pinto, *An Essay on Circulation and Credit,* trans. and annotated by the Rev. S. Baggs (London, 1774), 6. Fludyers also acted as warehousemen buying from other factors. (See Moir, "Gentlemen Clothiers," 233–234.) In the latter capacity they sold directly to export merchants. Sir Samuel was an M.P. from 1754 and eventually became a big government contractor and a "leading government financier." At his death in 1768 he was reputedly worth £900,000. Sir Lewis Namier and John Brooke, *The History of*

Parliament: the House of Commons 1754–1790, 3 vols. (Oxford, 1964), II, 442–444.

23. The letterbook (1763–1769) of Elderton & Hall is in the Somerset RO, DD/X/MSL (C679a), part 8. The records of Francis Hanson and Benjamin Mills are in PRO, C.113/16–18. The latter is described in Conrad Gill, "Blackwell Hall Factors, 1795–1799," *Economic History Review*, ser. 2, 6 (1953–54), 268–281.

24. See Somerset RO, DD/X/MSL (C/679a) pt. 8 to William Tree, 6, 13 Oct. 1768.

25. See PRO, C.113/18, pp. 497–499 to S. Heale, 13 June 1798.

26. Somerset RO, DD/X/MSL (C/679a) pt. 8. The references to purchasers are particularly numerous in letters to Thomas Bythesea (of Weak, near Trowbridge, Wilts.), beginning 6 Oct. 1768.

27. Ibid., to F. Arundel, 31 May 1764.

28. Ibid., to G. Walker, 27 Oct. 1763, and J. Walker, 19 Jan. 1764.

29. Ibid., to W. Turner, 16 June 1763, and to M. Withey, 22 Dec. 1768.

30. On notes, see, ibid., to G. Walker, 27 Oct., 3 Nov. 1763. These notes were issued by Blackwell Hall factors, not buyers. An act of 1697 required buyers of cloth to give their notes of hand to the factors for the use of the consigning clothiers who had manufactured the cloth. However, this act had fallen into neglect by 1739. Ephraim Lipson, *The Economic History of England*, 3d ed., 3 vols. (London, 1943), II, 26–30. Nevertheless Thomas Griggs, an Essex clothier, commonly received buyers' notes (of up to eight months' duration) for his crepes and says sold for him in London by Thomas Fenn "of Sudbury." K. H. Burley, "An Essex Clothier of the Eighteenth Century," *Economic History Review*, 2d ser., 11 (1958), 297–300. Fenn is also listed in the London directories as a warehouseman of Boar's Head Court, Gracechurch Street. The factor was bypassed.

31. For commission, see Somerset RO, DD/X/MSL (C/679a), Elderton & Hall to E. Eyres, 13 Oct. 1763, to Read & Wilkins, 3 Nov. 1763, to J. Walker, 9 Feb. 1764, and to J. Hooper, 7 June 1764. Cf. A. E. Bland, P. A. Brown, and R. H. Tawney, *English Economic History: Select Documents* (London, 1914), 493–494.

32. Somerset RO, DD/X/MSL (C/679a) pt. 8 to J. Cockell, 13, 20 Oct. 1768, and to W. Turner, 3 Nov. 1768.

33. PRO, C.113/18 to Chamberlain & Co., 29 Sept. 1795, and to W. Phelps, 1 Sept. 1798.

34. Ibid., to T. Clark, 1 June 1799, to W. Phelps, 15 June 1795, and to S. Heale, 13 June 1798.

35. R. G. Wilson, *Gentlemen Merchants: The Merchant Community in Leeds, 1700–1830* (Manchester and New York, 1971), 77–80. Some idea of the increasing weight of long credits in the Iberian and Italian markets at the end of the eighteenth century can be obtained by examining the growing credits owing from thence in the Kennaway Papers, Exeter RO, 58/9.

36. For the domestic trade generally, it was reported in the middle of the century: "The greatest Number of Country Dealers have 12 Months Credit, in fact, of the *London* Trader, for though many of them agree for 6 Months, yet as they keep constantly giving Orders, and send up Bills when it suits them, or are not drawn upon to the full Ballance, perhaps for 2 or 3 Years, the Accompt remaining open, it may be said that almost every Country Shopkeeper has Credit for a Year, if not more; for if the Tradesman in *London* does but receive sufficient for his Purpose, from Time to Time, and the Chapman continues to send him Orders, and deal regularly with him, and has a good Character . . . he thinks his Money safe in his Hands . . . Indeed, the *London* dealer in this Case, always thinks himself at Liberty to draw upon his Country Correspondent, for any Sum under the Ballance, when he has Occasion, and, if the Latter values his Credit, he will not be behind hand in paying his Draught." *The Tradesman's Director, or the London and Country Shopkeeper's Useful Companion* (London, 1756), 54–55.

37. If the export merchant was not free of the City of London, he could not buy in Blackwell Hall, though he could buy from a Blackwell Hall factor after the cloth had been exposed in the hall for three market days (one week). Merchants may have preferred buying from liveryman drapers or warehousemen to avoid legal complications. Maitland, *History of London,* I, 462–467.

38. On packers, see PRO, E.112/1236/3456 (London, Mich. Term, 29 Geo. II, Hamerton v. Vincent), E.112/1598/813 (London, Trin. Term, 6 Geo. III, de Errecarte v. Lynde), and E.112/1624/1597 (London, Mich. Term, 11 Geo. III, Baring v. Pugh); London Corporation RO, Mayor's Court, Equity bills, 1698–99, fol. 11, 1700–01, fol. 19; *Reasons for Preserving the Publick Market of Blackwell-Hall,*

and Restraining the Levant Company . . . (n.p., [1696?]); T. T[ryon], Merchant, *Some General Considerations Offered Relating to Our Present Trade* . . . (London, 1698), 14–15. The account books of Henry Hunter, Levant merchant of London, 1679–1698, show many cloth purchases from Robert Wandell, packer, for *ready money!* Berkshire RO, D/EZ5/B1, B3, B4. On packers, see also Westerfield, *Middlemen in English Business*, 312–314.

39. On the Halifax and Leeds factors, see Daniel Defoe, *A Tour thro' the Whole Island of Great Britain*, ed. G. D. H. Cole, 2 vols. (London, 1927), II, 605, 613–614; Herbert Heaton, *The Yorkshire Woollen and Worsted Industries*, 2d ed. (Oxford, 1965), 249, 271, 300, 382–385, 387–388; Westerfield, *Middleman in English Business*, 304–306; Wilson, *Gentlemen Merchants*, 82–83. In 1765, the big London Chesapeake firm of James Russell & Molleson employed the Halifax factor, John Winn, to make cloth purchases for them there. MdHS, MS 692.1 (Ridgely Papers), box vii, Winn to Charles Ridgely, 12 Mar. 1766. One Leeds factor, John Ellis, executed orders received directly from merchants in the Chesapeake. PRO, T.79/18.

40. Price, *Joshua Johnson's Letterbook*, nos. 14, 35, Johnson to firm, 17 Sept. 1771, 17 Apr. 1772; Richard Pares, "A London West-India Merchant House, 1740–1769," in R. Pares and A. J. P. Taylor, eds., *Essays Presented to Sir Lewis Namier* (London, 1956), 83–84. Cf. also W. H. B. Court, *The Rise of the Midland Industries, 1600–1838* (Oxford, 1938), 191–209.

41. Michael W. Flinn, *Men of Iron: The Crowleys in the Early Iron Industry*, Edinburgh University Publications: History, Philosophy, and Economics, no. 14 (Edinburgh, 1962), ch. 8.

42. For the six- and nine-month credits before 1772, see Carron Company letterbooks, SRO, GD 58/1/11, pp. 4–5, 53–54, 109–110, 144–145, and esp. 282. For later 12-month credit, see GD 58/1/13, pp. 438, 448–449, 454, 469, 490, 499, 516, 534, 548, 567, 589. Cf. also R. H. Campbell, *Carron Company* (Edinburgh, 1961), 104–114, 139; and Henry Hamilton, *An Economic History of Scotland in the Eighteenth Century* (Oxford, 1963), 193–200.

43. PRO, C.105/15 (Herne v. Baker), Elijah Chamberlain to James Hudson, Dublin, 10 Nov. 1733. See also L. M. Cullen, *Anglo-Irish Trade, 1660–1800* (Manchester, 1968), 95–98.

44. Price, *Joshua Johnson's Letterbook*, nos. 6, 41, Johnson to firm, 26 July 1771, 22 June 1772. Barclays' heavy involvement in

trade to Pennsylvania, New York, and the West Indies (in addition to their linendrapers' business) is confirmed in the 1784 winding-up ledger of D. & J. Barclay in Greater London RO, Barclay Perkins Papers.

45. Information supplied by Dr. Alastair J. Durie of the University of Aberdeen. See his book, *The Scottish Linen Industry in the Eighteenth Century* (Edinburgh, 1979). English buyers of Scottish linen could circumvent both Scottish merchants and London factors if they were prepared to offer Scottish manufacturers (putting-out masters) advantageous payment terms. John Wilson & Co. of Leeds ordered brown linen from eastern Scotland, which it finished at Leeds and sold all over northern England. It permitted its Scottish suppliers to draw thirty-day bills on its London correspondents immediately on shipment. Sheepscar Library, Leeds, Wilson Papers W/3/3, letterbook 1764–1773, to James Badenoch (Glamis), 20 Feb. 1768 and elsewhere in this and next volume. The Wilsons characteristically founded one of the earliest banks in Leeds.

46. Their function but not their finance is discussed in Westerfield, *Middlemen in English Business.*

47. [Daniel Defoe], *A Brief State of the Inland or Home Trade of England* (London, 1730), 21–22.

48. Guildhall Library, London, MS 8594 (Davison, Newman & Co. Grand Ledger), and MS 8630 (partnership contract, 1794). When the firm was reorganized in 1794, the partners' equity had grown to £207,968. There were, of course, much smaller wholesale grocers. Thomas Unwin and Thomas Fowle, citizens and grocers of London, commenced a wholesale and retail business in Gracechurch St. in 1707, selling sugar, raisins, currants, and spices, with a capital of £2,250, which rose to £3,600 by 1715. PRO, C.110/185 (Unwin v. Unwin).

49. London Corporation RO, Orphans' Court inventories, box 50.

50. Cullum's stock peaked at £48,000 in 1655, but this included his profits of office (excise) in the 1640s. Alan Simpson, *The Wealth of the Gentry, 1540–1660: East Anglian Studies* (Cambridge and Chicago, 1961), ch. 3. For the estate of a prosperous but smaller London draper withdrawing from trade, see Peter C. D. Brears, ed., *Yorkshire Probate Inventories, 1542–1689,* Yorkshire Archaeological Society, Record Series, CCXXIV, (n.p., 1972), 105–112.

51. A partnership contract of 25 Apr. 1763 between John Mount and Thomas Page, citizens and stationers of London, for continuing an existing business as stationers, booksellers, and printers, set the capital at £51,128. Each partner was permitted to take £12 a week or £624 p.a. from the business for personal (living) expenses. Berkshire RO, D/Emt B1.

52. A 1740 partnership contract for the firm of Basnett, Barrett & Newton, lacemen, St. Martin's-in-the-Fields, shows a capitalization of £7,000 for an entirely retail business, though one with aristocratic patronage. During the remainder of the century, the capital of the firm ranged from £4,000 to £12,000 as partners changed. Berkshire RO, D/EBt, B2–5, 8–10, 14. The partnership of James Alexander and Edward Fellowes, mercers, Bedford St., Covent Garden, started in 1702 with a capital of £4,500, which had risen to £7,635 in 1714 and £9,300 in 1723 when Fellowes retired. Alexander was also interested in a parallel firm with Henry Bostock, also in Covent Garden, which had a capital of £5,100 in 1721 and £9,000 in 1727. These were also retail firms with an aristocratic clientele. PRO, C.110/42, 43.

53. The firm of Holloway & Vines, carrying on a business in "Haberdashery and Linendrapery Wares" at Friday St., London, and Wootton-under-Edge, Gloucestershire, had a capital of £4,000 in 1735 and £5,064 in 1747. PRO, C.110/171(ii). Thomas Fletcher, a wealthy "girdler" of London left a personal estate in 1735 of £26,289, most of which was invested in "public securities" (£6,550), bonds (£8,043), and notes of hand (£2,024) and mortgages (£2,418); in addition he had a one-third share in a haberdashery partnership in Cheapside worth £6,633, implying that the net worth of the firm was £19,900. London Corporation RO, Orphans' Court inventories, box 51. His contemporary, John Seawell, a "leatherseller" of London, died in 1734 leaving a net personal estate of £4,909; he also had a one-third interest in a haberdashery partnership that produced £4,737 for the estate, implying that the net worth of that haberdashery firm was £14,210. Orphans' Court inventories, box 51. John Pocock, "haberdasher" of London, left a net personal estate of £11,483 in 1740, including a £4,037 share in a partnership, but this was not necessarily in haberdashery. Orphans' Court inventories, box 51. John White, a "haberdasher" in the hosiery trade, left a personal estate in 1732 in the vicinity of £10,000. Orphans' Court Inven-

tories, box 51. The firm of Blake & Paxton, mercers and warehousemen, Aldgate St., London, renewed their partnership in 1777 with a capital of £15,840. PRO, C.103/179. The Spitalsfield firm of Triquet, Van Sommer & Chavany, silk manufacturers and dealers, had a capital of £20,000 by their partnership contract of 1767. PRO, C.106/193(iii). Davies, Owen, Swanton & Co., hat-makers in Stockport, Cheshire, did their own distribution through their principal office in London. They had a capital of £12,050 in 1773 and (as Davies, Jones & Co.) £19,000 in 1785. One of the partners always lived in Bristol. Their correspondent, John Buchanan of Glasgow, distributed their full line there. PRO, C.107/104 (Frewer v. Davis).

54. London Corporation RO, Orphans' Court inventories, box 53, no. 62. On the Carys, see [Fairfax Harrison], *The Devon Carys*, 2 vols. (New York, 1920).

55. London Corporation RO, Orphans' Court inventories, box 50.

56. Ibid., box 51.

57. Ibid. Stanton & Thomas, glass-sellers, Poultry, London, had a capital of £2,460 in 1738, but it is not clear whether they had any export business. PRO, C.110/179.

58. National Westminster Bank archives, nos. 3967–3971, 3977–3980, Articles of partnership, Payne & Co., linendrapers, 1728–1764. When John Payne withdrew from the firm in 1764, he was declared entitled to £60,288, including £18,600 lent to the house; this implies that his one-half share in the capital was worth £41,688 and that the whole capital was £83,376. However, the former figure may have included current undistributed profits and interest on his loan.

59. Price, *Joshua Johnson's Letterbook*, no. 97a to firm, 9 Aug. 1773; PRO, E.144/27 (King v. Brown). Other bonds were signed by William Richardson, Cornhill, bookseller, Robert Porteous, Gracechurch St., woolendraper, and John Yarkery, Lombard St., hosier.

60. Bristol AO, 09476(2)–(7). The partners were Paul Fisher ($\frac{7}{12}$), Slade Baker ($\frac{4}{12}$), and William Griffin ($\frac{1}{12}$).

61. There are references to Fuhrer & Wagner in John Tarleton's accounts for 1761. Liverpool RO, 920 Tar 2/9. There is considerable documentation on this firm in PRO, C.108/287 (Fuhrer v. Thompson).

62. Based on experience of Lawson & Semple, e.g., the journal in SRO, RH 15/1200, 70–72, 85–86. SRA, TD111, is the journal (1765–1771) of Charles Paterson, a Glasgow linendraper selling to export merchants. His exact credit terms are not clear.

63. SRA, B10/15, no. 6852, and B10/12/2, fols. 23–24. Cf. also SRO, CC9/7/63 (1760, no. 69). On a smaller scale, the Chesapeake merchant James Dunlop had an $\frac{8}{25}$ interest in the firm of John Carlile & Co., warehousemen. See the partnership contract of 1760 in SRA, B10/15, no. 7511. There were a few independent warehouse concerns in Glasgow with capital close to that of the Cochrane concern. One was Archibald & John Coats, with a stock of £11,400 in 1760. SRA, B10/15, nos. 8354, 8358. (One of its partners, William Coats, later developed interests in the Chesapeake tobacco trade.) Another was the firm of Carmichaels & Scotts, with a capital of over £12,000 in 1771. SRO, CC9/7/68, pp. 291–295, 295–298.

64. Claims of James Dunlop and of James Wilson & Sons, PRO, A.O.13/28, 33. Contract of copartnery, McCall, Finlays & Scott, in SRA, B10/15, no. 7147. For other linen firms with Chesapeake merchant participation, see T. M. Devine, *The Tobacco Lords* (Edinburgh, 1975), 39.

65. PRO, C.107/104 (Frewer v. Davis), foreign letterbook, to J. Carter, 28 Apr. 1784, and to Peter Pegros, 9 Sept. 1784. Actually, the firm had sold on credit abroad before 1773, not always with happy results. See also Pares, "London West-India Merchant House," 84.

66. Cf. B. A. Holderness, "Credit in English Rural Society before the Nineteenth Century, with Special Reference to the Period 1650–1720," *Agricultural History*, 24 (1976), 97–109.

67. Josiah Child, *Brief Observations concerning Trade and Interest of Money* (London, 1668), 13, 15.

68. Charles Carlton, *The Court of Orphans* (Leicester, 1974), 47.

69. John Hope, *Letters on Credit*, 2d ed. (London, 1784), 9–10 (originally published in Woodfall's *Public Advertiser*). On the inability of exporting merchants in French ports to obtain long credits, see Yale University Library, Jonathan Williams letterbook 4, pp. 216–217, Williams to Crockett & Harris, 28 Sept. 1783.

70. On James Braine, see PRO, E.112/980/264 (London, Mich. Term, 2 Geo. I, Braine v. Norton), and E.112/987/708 (London, Mich. Term, 6 Geo. I, Braine v. Hitchcock). On Benjamin and

James Braine, see D. W. Jones, "London Overseas-Merchant Groups at the End of the Seventeenth Century and the Moves against the East India Company" (D.Phil. diss., Oxford, 1970), 420–422, 433–436, 465–467. The same source shows Michael Jones & Co. and John Marsh also importing both tobacco and linen in London in 1694–1696.

71. Based on the account books of Joshua Johnson, MdHR, particularly Private Accounts 1513–1519. Since tobacco was of relatively low density, tobacco ships homeward bound from the Chesapeake required some ballast, usually iron from the 1730s on.

72. The London directories, 1763–1765, also list Salmon & Slade as "wholesale Haberdashers & Tobacconists."

73. Based on the London directories and on "shop notes" and accounts of sale in the various American merchant or planter collections already cited. The ledgers of Joshua Johnson are particularly useful (MdHR).

74. At first glance, there is no reason why credit should in the long run have increased aggregate demand for British goods in America—even if it did so in the short run or for unusually expensive items (such as coaches). However, insofar as consumer credit permitted propertyless men to rent farms that otherwise would have gone unrented, or larger planters to divert resources (particularly liquid resources) to buying slaves and servants or improving land, consumer credit did help increase production and income and the demand for imported goods. See chapter 7.

75. Assuming half the goods to have been exported on commission (either as cargoes or planter's orders) without a profit margin, and the other half to have been exported and sold overseas on the merchant's own account with an average profit margin of 40 percent, I get an average profit margin on all exports of 20 percent. See appendix A.

7 THE SIGNIFICANCE OF CREDIT IN THE CHESAPEAKE AND THE FINANCIAL CRISIS OF 1772

1. See appendix A for some explanation of contemporary usage regarding markups or advances. On the number of firms in the trade, see PRO, P.R.O.30/8/343; Northampton RO, Fitzwilliam-Burke MSS, A.xxv.74; Jacob M. Price, ed., *Joshua Johnson's Letter-book, 1771–1774: Letters from a Merchant in London to His Partners in*

Maryland, London Record Society, XV (London, 1979), no. 161. A "cash market" included any sales payable within thirty days, or within sixty days if secured by bill or note.

2. W. L. Clements Library, Ann Arbor, C. Townshend Papers, old no. VIII/24A/29, Archibald Henderson to [?], Jermyn St., 25 Jan. 1766.

3. On the Cuninghame claim after 1790, see PRO, T.79/1.

4. Peter J. Coleman, *Debtors and Creditors in America . . . 1607–1900* (Madison, Wis., 1974), chs. 12 and 14.

5. See source in note 2.

6. A. C. Land, "Economic Behavior in a Planting Society," *Journal of Southern History,* 33 (1967), 479.

7. On the "cargo trade," see Jacob M. Price, "One Family's Empire," *Maryland Historical Magazine,* 72 (1977), 176–179, 185–189; MdHS, MS 692.1 (Ridgely Papers), box vii, J. Russell to Capt. C. Ridgely, 7 Jan., 3 Mar., 4 Sept. 1766; C. Ridgely to Russell, 13 Nov. 1766; box ix, W. Molleson to C. Ridgely, 21 Aug. 1770; Coutts & Co. archives, London, James Russell Papers, VI, James Forbes to Russell, 21 Feb., 27 June, 31 Aug. 1774; New York Historical Society, W. Lux letterbook, to J. Russell, 3 Nov. 1766; MdHS, Aquila Hall letterbook, Christopher Court & Co. to A. Hall, 1 Aug. 1772; MdHS, H. Hollyday Papers, W. Anderson to J. Hollyday, 29 Apr. 1765, 6 May 1767; LC, Galloway Papers, IV, fol. 8640, S. Grove to S. Galloway, 10 Oct. 1761; and appendix C.

8. Cf. *Hastie and Jamieson v. Robert Arthur* (1770), printed House of Lords appeal case, in New York Public Library, Arents Collection.

9. References scattered throughout printed correspondence of Dr. Charles Carroll in *Maryland Historical Magazine;* see, e.g., 18 (1923), 336–337, and 19 (1924), 184–186, 286. There also appears to have been a system by which the London merchant "consigned" goods to the Chesapeake merchant to be sold on commission. Cf. LC, Galloway Papers, Higginson & Bird letterbook, no. 1867 to C. Fleming, 24 Dec. 1718.

10. VaHS, Adams MSS (N-Y), Thomas Adams to Perkins, Buchanan & Brown, 22 March 1770 (draft).

11. Colonial Williamsburg, Norton MSS, nos. 4, 17, J. Norton to J. H. Norton, 25 Jan. 1769, 4 Sept. 1773. Mrs. Mason refers to a list of 398 debtors owing the Norton firm £63,856 in 1773, but she

does not print it, date it, or cite its location. Frances Norton Mason, ed., *John Norton & Sons, Merchants of London and Virginia* (Richmond, Va., 1937), 293.

12. Price, "One Family's Empire," 196–197, 211.

13. *Historical Statistics of the United States* (1976), II, 1189–91.

14. On prices, see Jacob M. Price, *France and the Chesapeake*, 2 vols. (Ann Arbor, Mich., 1973), I, 671–677. For the crisis of 1772, see ibid., I, 639–643, 696–700; Price, "One Family's Empire," 186–189; Henry Hamilton, "The Failure of the Ayr Bank, 1772," *Economic History Review*, 2d ser., 8 (1956), 405–417; idem, *An Economic History of Scotland in the Eighteenth Century* (Oxford, 1963), 317–325; L. S. Sutherland, "Sir George Colebrook's World Corner in Alum, 1771–3," *Economic History: A Supplement of the Economic Journal*, 3 (1936), 237–258; Charles Wilson, *Anglo-Dutch Commerce and Finance* (Cambridge, 1941), 169–182; Richard B. Sheridan, "The British Credit Crisis of 1772," *Journal of Economic History*, 20 (1960), 161–186.

15. The following account is based primarily upon the Joshua Johnson letterbook I in the MdHR (Private Accounts, 1507), particularly the letters to Johnson's partners between June 1772 and December 1773—the most detailed account of the way the American merchants and warehousemen of London reacted to the crisis. Most have been published in Price, *Joshua Johnson's Letterbook*. Cf. also Jacob M. Price, "Joshua Johnson in London," in Anne Whiteman et al., *Statesmen, Scholars and Merchants* (Oxford, 1973), 153–180, reprinted in revised form as introduction to *Joshua Johnson's Letterbook*; and LC, W. Reynolds letterbook, pp. 32–33, to J. Norton, 8 Feb. 1773.

16. T. S. Ashton, *An Economic History of England: The 18th Century* (London, 1955), 254. Much lower (and presumably erroneous?) totals for the early 1770s are given in the *London Chronicle*, 64 (30 Oct.–1 Nov. 1788).

17. *Gentleman's Magazine*, 42 (1772), 344, 392.

18. PRO, Ind. 22634–53 (B.4/1–20), Court of Bankruptcy Docket Books. The biggest bankruptcy after 1720 was probably Buchanan & Hamilton of London (1752). Their assignees were Samuel Rickards of Fenchurch St., haberdasher, and Jasper Mauduit, Israel Mauduit, Thomas Wright, and John Philibrown, of Cullum St., warehousemen. Mauduit, Wright & Co. appear to

have been the leading warehousemen supplying the North American trade with woolens.

19. This procedure is explained in some detail in Joshua Johnson's letterbook (see note 15), on which the following two paragraphs are based. For Russell, see also Price, "One Family's Empire," 186–189. For Buchanan, see also PRO, A.O.13/60, fol. 156, and A.O.12/6, fol. 109. For Bland's failure, owing £50,000, see VaHS, Lee Papers, W. Lee to R. H. Lee, 29 Feb. 1772; Colonial Williamsburg, Norton MSS, J. Norton to J. H. Norton, 30 Apr. 1773.

20. See note 6.

21. Emory G. Evans, "Planter Indebtedness and the Coming of the Revolution in Virginia," *William and Mary Quarterly,* 3d ser., 19 (1962), 511–533.

22. On Maryland, see Richard Arthur Overfield, "The Loyalists of Maryland during the American Revolution" (Ph.D. diss., University of Maryland, 1968).

23. Sheridan, "British Credit Crisis." Without a computer, Sheridan attempted a breakdown of the size distribution of the larger debts. He did not, however, explain his principles of selection, nor could he attempt a functional analysis. Nevertheless, he did point out that "at least fifty-five of the individuals from whom £500 or more was claimed [after the war] were members of the house of Burgesses from 1769 to 1774." Ibid., 183.

24. Land, "Economic Behavior," 477.

25. Farell & Jones claim, PRO, T.79/9, and Somerset RO, DD/GC 62.

26. Gale claim, PRO, T.79/21.

27. Lyde claim, PRO, T.79/100A.

28. Mildred claim, PRO, T.79/26.

29. Gist claim, PRO, T.79/31.

30. Speirs claim, PRO, T.79/40.

31. MdHR, Red Books, XXIII, 86:1,2, and XXVI, 31; PRO, A.O.13/92, fols. 425–426. See also Price, "One Family's Empire," 201–202.

8 THE IMPLICATIONS FOR BRITISH INDUSTRIAL AND COMMERCIAL DEVELOPMENT

1. T. S. Ashton, *An Economic History of England: The 18th Century* (London, 1955), 27–29, 41, 84; idem, *Economic Fluctuations in*

England, 1700–1800 (Oxford, 1959), 86–88; idem, *The Industrial Revolution* (London, 1948), 7–11.

2. Norman Sydney Buck, *The Development of the Organisation of Anglo-American Trade, 1800–1850* (New Haven, Conn., 1925), esp. 131–151; Ray B. Westerfield, *Early History of American Auctions: A Chapter in Commercial History*, Transactions of the Connecticut Academy of Arts and Sciences, 23 (New Haven, Conn., 1920), 159–210, esp. 172–179.

3. For a good introduction to the literature on this subject, see François Crouzet, ed., *Capital Formation in the Industrial Revolution* (London, 1972), particularly the contributions of F. Crouzet and S. Pollard; M. M. Edwards, *The Growth of the British Cotton Trade, 1780–1815* (Manchester, 1967), esp. chs. 9 and 10; Seymour Shapiro, *Capital and the Cotton Industry in the Industrial Revolution* (Ithaca, N.Y., 1967); S. D. Chapman, *The Early Factory Masters* (Newton Abbot, 1967), 18–26, 125–144; idem, "Financial Restraints on the Growth of Firms in the Cotton Industry, 1790–1850," *Economic History Review*, 2d ser., 32 (1979), 50–69.

4. Virginia D. Harrington, *The New York Merchant on the Eve of the Revolution* (New York, 1935), 92–93; Arthur L. Jensen, *The Maritime Commerce of Colonial Philadelphia* (Madison, Wis., 1963), 123–124; Philip L. White, *The Beekmans of New York in Politics and Commerce, 1647–1877* (New York, 1956), 245, 261, 415, 423, 456–457, 504, 517; idem, ed., *The Beekman Mercantile Papers, 1746–1799*, 3 vols. (New York, 1956), I, 92, 134, 139–140, 207, 287–288, 322, 345–346, 350, 379, 478, II, 839, 851, 867, 939, 1023, 1055–56, 1065, 1074, 1119, 1173, 1283; Philip M. Hamer et al., eds., *The Papers of Henry Laurens*, 7 vols. (Columbia, S. C., 1968–1979), I, 101, 113, 125, 126, 167, 251, 290, II, 58–59, 67, 136, 147, 270–271, 306–307, 405, 463, 487–488, III, 126, 363, 464, 494, IV, 76, 97, 185, 276, 290, 413, 436–437, 536, 540, 547, V, 281, 605, 637, 653, 710, VI, 406, VII, 144, 257–258, 429–430, 452–453. In addition, sugar, molasses, rum, coffee, and indigo from the West Indies were frequently sold at auction (after ca. 1748) in both Charleston and New York. *Beekman Papers*, I, 21, 49, 50, 54, 64, 254, 437; *Laurens Papers*, II, 267–268, 316, 370, 382, 519, III, 149, 209, 251, 395, 473, 488, 505, 513, IV, 28, 84, 182, 214, 215, VII, 371. Prize goods, of course, were regularly sold at auction.

Appendix A MARKUPS AND PROFIT MARGINS
IN THE CHESAPEAKE TRADE

1. Jacob M. Price, ed., *Joshua Johnson's Letterbook, 1771–1774: Letters from a Merchant in London to His Partners in Maryland*, London Record Society, XV (London, 1979), no. 122a, Johnson to firm, 19 Feb. 1774.

2. See PRO, C.104/145 (Jackson v. Neames), Thomas Lyttleton to John Neames Jr. (London), Annapolis, 23 Sept. 1762, 27 Aug. 1763, 8 Mar. 1764; PRO, H.C.A.30/258/287, T. to E. West, 12 Nov. 1756; SRO, R.H.15/1179 (Court of Session, Unextracted Processes, Currie Dal. 20/2, no. 15/10), J. Lawson to J. Semple, 21 Jan. 1764.

Select Bibliography

MANUSCRIPTS

BRITISH AND IRISH LIBRARIES AND ARCHIVES

Bristol

BRISTOL ARCHIVES OFFICE

Fisher, Slade & Griffin partnership contracts (90476/2−7)
Harford Family Papers
Mark Harford ledger A
John King Papers (08841/1−7)
Henry Woolnough account book (AC/W03/1)

Carlisle

CUMBRIA RECORD OFFICE

Lonsdale Papers

Cork

LIBRARY OF UNIVERSITY COLLEGE, CORK

Samuel Hoare Ledger and Journal (MSS 31, 31A) (Photocopy
in National Library of Ireland, Dublin)

Edinburgh

NATIONAL LIBRARY OF SCOTLAND

Fettercairn Papers (acc. 4796), boxes 199, 200, 201, 212, and
215. Accounts of Sir William Forbes, James Hunter & Co.
Mure Papers (MS 4942)
Oswald Papers

SCOTTISH RECORD OFFICE

C.C.9/7/62–68. Glasgow Commissary Court. Register of Testaments

C.C.9/16. Glasgow Commissary Court. Register of Deeds. Warrants of the Commissary

C.S.96. Court of Session. Unextracted Processes (business records presented as exhibits in law suits)

C.S.230, 231. Court of Sessions. Unextracted Processes (bills and answers in suits)

C.S.230, 231 Sequestrations. Court of Sessions bankruptcy papers

E.504 Scottish port books

G.D.58/1/11–13. Carron Company letterbooks

R.D.2, 3, 4. Court of Sessions. Register of Deeds

R.H.15/1179–1200. Unextracted Processes. Lawson & Semple accounts (recently renumbered as C.S.96)

Exeter

EXETER RECORD OFFICE

Thomas Jeffery Papers (61/6/1)
Kennaway Collection (58/9)
Samuel Milford journal (71/8)

Glasgow

LANARKSHIRE SHERIFF COURT

Register of Deeds

MITCHELL LIBRARY

Papers of Daniel Campbell of Shawfield
Steggall-Bogle Papers. Journal of John Brown of Waterhaughs

STRATHCLYDE REGIONAL ARCHIVES

B10/15. Glasgow Burgh Court. Register of Deeds

TD 111. Journal of Charles Paterson

TD 131. Speirs Accounts

TD 132/1–72. Holmes, McKillop deposit. J. H. Kippen deed box

TD 161-1. Ship Bank Balance Book, 1752–1761 (copy)

TD 219/9/2(1). Campbell of Succoth Papers

T-MJ 1,3. Mitchell, Johnson & Co. deposit. Ledgers of T. & A. Grahame, solicitors

T-MJ 79. Baird, Hay & Co. journal

T-MJ 108. Estate Papers of James Somervell of Hamilton Farm

T-MJ 422. George Pagan & Co. partnership papers

Leeds

SHEEPSCAR LIBRARY

Wilson Papers

Liverpool

LIVERPOOL RECORD OFFICE

Tarleton Papers (920)

London

BRITISH LIBRARY

Add. MSS 33,030. Newcastle American Papers. Commons Committee of 1766

Add. MSS 44,998, 45,022. Russell family of Birmingham

CORPORATION RECORD OFFICE

Mayor's Court. Equity bills and answers

Orphans' Court. Inventories, boxes 29, 37, 39, 42, 49–56

FRIENDS HOUSE LIBRARY (EUSTON)

Gurney Papers

GREATER LONDON RECORD OFFICE, LONDON SECTION (COUNTY HALL)

Barclay Perkins Papers. Winding-up ledger of D. & J. Barclay, ca. 1784–1790

GREATER LONDON RECORD OFFICE, MIDDLESEX SECTION (DARTMOUTH ST.)

Eliot Family Papers (acc. 1017)

GUILDHALL LIBRARY

Davison, Newman & Co. records (8594, 8630)

PUBLIC RECORD OFFICE

A.O.12 and 13. Audit Office. Claims (ca. 1776–1789) of loyalist émigrés and other British sufferers during the Revolutionary War

B.4/1–20. Court of Bankruptcy. Docket Books

C.103–8, 110–111, 113. Chancery Masters' Exhibits

C.217/86/1–3. Chancery. Petty Bag Office. George Tarbutt & Sons records

C.O.5/1305. Board of Trade. Original Correspondence, Virginia

E.112. Exchequer (Equity Side). Bills and Answers

E.144. Exchequer. Extents and Inquisitions

E.190. Exchequer. Port Books

H.C.A.30/258. Admiralty Court. Intercepted Correspondence

Prob.3, 4, and 5. Prerogative Court of Canterbury, Inventories

Prob.11. Prerogative Court of Canterbury, Wills. (Items listed in the notes under their P.C.C. numbers only were examined before transfer from Somerset House to the PRO.)

P.R.O.30/8. Chatham Papers, including those of William Pitt the younger

T.1. Treasury In-Papers

T.79. Treasury. Claims (ca. 1795–1811) of British subjects for unrecoverable pre-1776 American debts

Maidstone
KENT ARCHIVES OFFICE

U513/B1. Bosworth & Griffith partnership papers

Northampton
NORTHAMPTONSHIRE RECORD OFFICE

Fitzwilliam-Burke MS A.xxv.74. Tobacco imports, 1775

Norwich
NORFOLK AND NORWICH RECORD OFFICE

Gurney Family Papers (RQG 296–302, 485–487, 495–497, 505–507, 542–543, 546–547)

Preston
LANCASHIRE RECORD OFFICE

DDX/632/1. Sir Ellis Cunliffe estate papers

Reading
BERKSHIRE RECORD OFFICE

D/EBt B2–5, 8–10, 14. Basnett, Barrett & Newton records

D/EC/B2. Craven & Parker partnership contract

D/EM/B18. Charles & Joseph Hatt papers
D/Emt/B1. Mount & Page partnership contract
D/EZ5/B1, B3, B4. Henry Hunter account books

Taunton
SOMERSET RECORD OFFICE

DD/X/MSL (C679a), pt. 8. Elderton & Hall letterbook

BRITISH PRIVATE AND INSTITUTIONAL HOLDINGS

Blairquhan, Ayrshire
MUNIMENTS OF SIR JAMES HUNTER BLAIR, BART.

Ledger and journal of Sir James Hunter Blair, 1st Bart.

Cavens, Kirkbean, Kirkcudbrightshire
MUNIMENTS OF MAJOR R. A. OSWALD

Correspondence of Richard Oswald (1705–1784)

Edinburgh
BANK OF SCOTLAND

Court of Directors Minute Books, III, IV

ROYAL BANK OF SCOTLAND

Court of Directors Minute Books, I–V

London
BANK OF ENGLAND. SECRETARY'S OFFICE

Bank Court Minutes

BANK OF ENGLAND. BANK RECORD OFFICE, ROEHAMPTON

Drawing Office ledgers

BARCLAYS BANK LTD., HEAD OFFICE, LOMBARD ST., VAULTS

Annual balances, 1748–1799
Discount books, 1769–1774

BARCLAYS BANK ARCHIVES, MARTINS BANK SECTION, LOMBARD ST.

Martin & Co.: discount book, 1731–1735; trial balance book, 1731–1744; Christmas balance book, 1742–1748, 1755–1760; general balance book, 1746–1752; ledger, 1770–1772

COUTTS & CO., STRAND. ARCHIVES

James Russell Papers

GLYN, MILLS & CO. (NOW PART OF WILLIAMS' & GLYN'S BANK, LTD.)
ARCHIVES

Hallifax, Mills, Glyn & Mitton Christmas Book, 1774
Mason, Currie, James & Yallowley, "Banking Stock Book,"
1774

NATIONAL WESTMINSTER BANK, LTD. ARCHIVES

"Bristol Old Bank" (Lloyd, Elton, Miller, Tyndall, Gillam &
Edye), General balance book, 1772–1782
Payne & Co., linendrapers: partnership contracts, 1728–1764
(nos. 3967–3971, 3977–3980)
Prescotts, Grote, Culverden & Hollingworth, bankers: list of
customers, 1766; partnership agreements of 1776 and 1792;
summary book, 1780–1865
Smith & Payne, bankers: partnerships of 1758–1788 and related papers (nos. 2245, 3981–82, 4559); Abel Smith's letterbook; Nottingham balance, 30 Dec. 1780
Staples, Baron Dimsdale, Son & Co., index and ledger, 1774–
1775

AMERICAN REPOSITORIES

Annapolis, Md.
HALL OF RECORDS

Private Accounts 1507–1519. Joshua Johnson letterbooks,
journals, ledgers
Red Books, xxiii, xxvi (on loyalist property)

Ann Arbor, Mich.
WILLIAM L. CLEMENTS LIBRARY

Charles Townshend Papers

Baltimore, Md.
MARYLAND HISTORICAL SOCIETY

Aquila Hall Papers
H. Hollyday Papers
Horsey (Lee) Deposit
Ridgely Family Papers

Chapel Hill, N.C.
UNIVERSITY OF NORTH CAROLINA LIBRARY. SOUTHERN HISTORICAL COLLECTIONS

C. W. Dabney Papers

New Haven, Conn.
YALE UNIVERSITY LIBRARY

Jonathan Williams letterbooks

New York
NEW YORK HISTORICAL SOCIETY

William Lux letterbook

NEW YORK PUBLIC LIBRARY

Custis MSS

Richmond, Va.
VIRGINIA HISTORICAL SOCIETY

Adams Family Papers
Custis Family Papers
Lee Family Papers. Correspondence
Lee (Ludwell) Papers. Green Spring Estate Papers
George Washington's accounts and papers on Custis estate
(MS 5:3 W277, 1, 2)

VIRGINIA STATE LIBRARY

Allason Papers
John Norton & Son: cash book, sales book

San Marino, Calif.
HENRY E. HUNTINGTON LIBRARY

Tinsley MSS (BR, box 16)

Washington, D.C.
LIBRARY OF CONGRESS. MANUSCRIPTS DIVISION

J. Custis letterbook and papers
Galloway Papers
Galloway Papers. Higginson & Bird letterbook
Neil Jamieson Papers
Jones Family Papers

R. Pleasants letterbook
W. Reynolds letterbook

Williamsburg, Va.

COLLEGE OF WILLIAM AND MARY LIBRARY

Jerdone Papers. William Johnston's ledger F and letterbook

COLONIAL WILLIAMSBURG FOUNDATION

Norton Papers

PRINTED MATERIALS
CONTEMPORARY PUBLICATIONS AND
OTHER PRIMARY SOURCES

Bland, A. E., P. A. Brown, and R. H. Tawney, eds. *English Economic History: Select Documents.* London, 1914.

Campbell, Richard. *The London Tradesman.* London [1741]; reprinted 1969.

Carlyle, Alexander. *Autobiography of the Rev. Dr. Alexander Carlyle.* Edinburgh and London, 1860.

Carroll, Dr. Charles. "Extracts from Account and Letter Books of Dr. Charles Carroll of Annapolis," *Maryland Historical Magazine,* 18 (1923), 197–233, 323–341; 19 (1924), 179–192, 283–303, 393–400; 27 (1932), 215–230, 314–334.

Carroll, Charles, Barrister. "Letters of Charles Carroll, Barrister," ed. W. Stull Holt, *Maryland Historical Magazine,* 32 (1937), 35–46, 174–190, 348–368.

Carter, Landon. *The Diary of Colonel Landon Carter of Sabine Hall, 1752–1778,* ed. Jack P. Greene. 2 vols. Charlottesville, Va., 1965.

The Case of the Planters of Tobacco in Virginia . . . To Which is Added, A Vindication of the said Representation. London, 1733.

Champion, Richard. *Considerations on the Present Situation of Great Britain and the United States of America,* 2d ed. London, 1784.

Child, Josiah. *Brief Observations concerning Trade and Interest of Money.* London, 1668.

The Clothiers Complaint: or, Reasons for Passing the Bill against the Blackwell-Hall Factors. London, 1692.

The Clothiers Reasons for Petitioning the Commons of Great Britain . . . to Oblige all Buyers of Cloth upon Credit to Give Notes . . . N.p. [1714].

Considerations Relating to the Tobacco Trade at London, so Far as It Relates to the Merchants Who are Factors. [London, 1733].

[Defoe, Daniel]. *A Brief State of the Inland or Home Trade of England.* London, 1730.

Defoe, Daniel. *A Tour thro' the Whole Island of Great Britain,* ed. G. D. H. Cole. 2 vols. London, 1927.

Dum Spiro Spero [pseud.]. *An Humble Representation of the State of our Woollen Manufactures.* London, 1700.

Hope, John. *Letters on Credit.* 2d ed. London, 1784.

Jefferson, Thomas. *The Papers of Thomas Jefferson,* ed. Julian P. Boyd. Princeton, N.J., 1950– .

Johnson, Joshua. *Joshua Johnson's Letterbook, 1771–1774: Letters from a Merchant in London to His Partners in Maryland,* ed. Jacob M. Price. London Record Society, XV. London, 1979.

Laurens, Henry. *The Papers of Henry Laurens,* ed. Philip M. Hamer et al. 7 vols. Columbia, S.C., 1968–1979.

Macpherson, David. *Annals of Commerce, Manufactures, Fisheries and Navigation.* 4 vols. London, 1805.

Maitland, William. *The History of London.* 2 vols. London, 1756.

Mason, Frances Norton, ed. *John Norton & Sons, Merchants of London and Virginia.* Richmond, Va., 1937.

Mure, William, of Caldwell, ed. *Selections from the Family Papers Preserved at Caldwell.* Maitland Club. Glasgow, 1854.

Pinto, Isaac de. *An Essay on Circulation and Credit,* trans. and annotated by the Rev. S. Baggs. London, 1774.

Reasons for Preserving the Publick Market of Blackwell-Hall. N.p. [ca. 1696].

Reasons for Preserving the Publick Market of Blackwell-Hall, and Restraining the Levant Company . . . N.p. [1696?].

A Reply to the Vindication of the Representation of the Case of the Planters of Tobacco in a Letter to Sir J[ohn] R[andolph]. London, 1733.

The Tradesman's Director, or the London and Country Shopkeeper's Useful Companion. London, 1756.

Treloar, Sir William Purdie. *A Lord Mayor's Diary, 1906–7 to which is Added the Official Diary of Micajah Perry Lord Mayor, 1738–9.* London, 1920.

T[ryon], T. *Some General Considerations Offered Relating to Our Present Trade . . .* London, 1698.

White, Philip L., ed. *The Beekman Mercantile Papers, 1746–1799.* 3 vols. New York, 1956.

Contemporary London Periodicals

The Free Briton (1733)
Gentleman's Magazine (1772)
London Chronicle (1788)
Political State of Great Britain (1735)

Printed Cases in Legal Appeals

Court of Sessions, Edinburgh
  Collection in Signet Library, Edinburgh
House of Lords, London
  Hastie and Jamieson v. Robert Arthur (1770), in New York Public Library, Arents Collection
  John M'Dowall et al. v. Mrs. James Ferguson als McMikin (1783)
  Estate of Humphrey Morice (1720s), in BL, 515.1.15 (106–112)
  de Ron v. Vaneck, in BL, 515.1.15 (14)

MODERN MONOGRAPHS AND
OTHER SECONDARY ACCOUNTS

Anderson, B. L. "The Attorney and the Early Capital Market in Lancashire," in J. B. Harris, ed., *Liverpool and Merseyside: Essays in the Economic and Social History of the Port and Its Hinterland*, pp. 50–77. London, 1969.
——— "Money and the Structure of Credit in the Eighteenth Century," *Business History*, 12 (1970), 85–101.
——— "Provincial Aspects of the Financial Revolution of the Eighteenth Century," *Business History*, 11 (1969), 11–22.
Ashton, Thomas S. *Economic Fluctuations in England, 1700–1800*. Oxford, 1959.
——— *An Economic History of England: The 18th Century*. London, 1955.
——— *The Industrial Revolution*. London, 1948.
Barclay, Charles W., et al. *A History of the Barclay Family*. 3 vols. London, 1924–1934.
Buck, Norman Sydney. *The Development of the Organisation of Anglo-American Trade, 1800–1850*. New Haven, Conn., 1925.
Buist, Marten G. *At Spes Non Fracta: Hope & Co., 1770–1815: Merchant Bankers and Diplomats at Work*. The Hague, 1974.
Burley, K. H. "An Essex Clothier of the Eighteenth Century," *Economic History Review*, 2d ser., 11 (1958), 289–301.
Cameron, Rondo, et al. *Banking in the Early Stages of Industrialization*. New York, 1967.

Campbell, R. H. *Carron Company*. Edinburgh, 1961.

Carlton, Charles. *The Court of Orphans*. Leicester, 1974.

Cave, Charles H. *A History of Banking in Bristol from 1750 to 1899*. Bristol, 1899.

Chapman, Stanley D. *The Early Factory Masters: The Transition to the Factory System in the Midlands Textile Industry*. Newton Abbot, 1967.

―――― "Financial Restraints on the Growth of Firms in the Cotton Industry, 1790–1850," *Economic History Review*, 2d ser., 32 (1979), 50–69.

Checkland, Sidney G. *Scottish Banking: A History*. Glasgow, 1975.

Clapham, Sir John. *The Bank of England*. 2 vols. Cambridge, 1944.

Clarke, M. L. *George Grote: A Biography*. London, 1962.

Coleman, Donald C. *Sir John Banks: Baronet and Businessman*. Oxford, 1963.

Coleman, Peter J. *Debtors and Creditors in America . . . 1607–1900*. Madison, Wis., 1974.

Court, William H. B. *The Rise of the Midland Industries, 1600–1838*. Oxford, 1938.

Crouzet, François, ed. *Capital Formation in the Industrial Revolution*. London, 1972.

Cullen, Louis M. *Anglo-Irish Trade, 1660–1800*. Manchester, 1968.

Davis, Ralph. "English Foreign Trade, 1660–1700," *Economic History Review*, 2d ser., 7 (1954), 150–166.

―――― "English Foreign Trade, 1700–1774," *Economic History Review*, 2d ser., 15 (1962), 285–303.

―――― *The Rise of the English Shipping Industry in the Seventeenth and Eighteenth Centuries*. London, 1962.

Devine, Thomas M. "Sources of Capital for the Glasgow Tobacco Trade, c. 1740–1780," *Business History*, 16 (1974), 113–129.

―――― *The Tobacco Lords: A Study of the Tobacco Merchants of Glasgow and Their Trading Activities*. Edinburgh, 1975.

Dickson, Peter G. M. *The Financial Revolution in England*. London, 1967.

―――― *The Sun Insurance Office, 1710–1960*. London, 1960.

Donnan, Elizabeth M. "Eighteenth Century Merchants: Micajah Perry," *Journal of Economic and Business History*, 4 (1931), 70–98.

Durie, Alastair J. *The Scottish Linen Industry in the Eighteenth Century*. Edinburgh, 1979.

Edwards, Michael M. *The Growth of the British Cotton Trade, 1780–1815*. Manchester, 1967.

Ernst, Joseph A. "Genesis of the Currency Act of 1764: Virginia Paper Money and the Protection of British Investments," *William and Mary Quarterly*, 3d ser., 22 (1965), 33–74.

────── *Money and Politics in Early America, 1755–1775: A Study of the Currency Act of 1764 and the Political Economy of Revolution.* Chapel Hill, N.C., 1973.

Evans, Emory G. "Planter Indebtedness and the Coming of the Revolution in Virginia," *William and Mary Quarterly*, 3d ser., 19 (1962), 511–533.

Ferguson, E. James. "Currency Finance: An Interpretation of Colonial Monetary Practices," *William and Mary Quarterly*, 3d ser., 10 (1953), 153–180.

Fisher, H. E. S. *The Portugal Trade: A Study of Anglo-Portuguese Commerce 1700–1770.* London, 1971.

Flinn, Michael W. *Men of Iron: The Crowleys in the Early Iron Industry.* Edinburgh University Publications: History, Philosophy, and Economics, no. 14. Edinburgh, 1962.

Gill, Conrad. "Blackwell Hall Factors, 1795–1799," *Economic History Review*, 2d ser., 6 (1953–54), 268–281.

Gipson, Lawrence H. "Virginia Planter Debts before the American Revolution," *Virginia Magazine of History and Biography*, 69 (1961), 259–277.

Grassby, Richard. "English Merchant Capitalism in the Late Seventeenth Century: The Composition of Business Fortunes," *Past & Present*, no. 46 (1970), 87–107.

────── "The Personal Wealth of the Business Community in Seventeenth Century England," *Economic History Review*, 2d ser., 23 (1970), 220–234.

────── "The Rate of Profit in Seventeenth Century England," *English Historical Review*, 84 (1969), 721–751.

Gray, Stanley, and Vertrees Judson Wyckoff. "The International Tobacco Trade in the Seventeenth Century," *Southern Economic Journal*, 7 (1940), 1–26.

Grote, Harriet Lewin. *The Personal Life of George Grote*, 2d ed. London, 1873.

Hamilton, Henry. *An Economic History of Scotland in the Eighteenth Century.* Oxford, 1963.

────── "The Failure of the Ayr Bank, 1772," *Economic History Review*, 2d ser., 8 (1956), 405–417.

Harrell, Isaac S. *Loyalism in Virginia.* Durham, N.C., 1926.

—— "Some Neglected Phases of the Revolution in Virginia," *William and Mary Quarterly*, 2d ser., 5 (1925), 159–170.

Harrington, Virginia D. *The New York Merchant on the Eve of the Revolution*. New York, 1935.

[Harrison, Fairfax]. *The Devon Carys*. 2 vols. New York, 1920.

Heaton, Herbert. *The Yorkshire Woollen and Worsted Industries*, 2d ed. Oxford, 1965.

Hemphill, John M. "Freight Rates in the Maryland Tobacco Trade, 1707–1762," *Maryland Historical Magazine*, 54 (1959), 36–58, 153–187.

Holderness, B. A. "Credit in English Rural Society before the Nineteenth Century, with Special Reference to the Period 1650–1720," *Agricultural History*, 24 (1976), 97–109.

Hughes, Edward. *North Country Life in the Eighteenth Century*, vol. II, *Cumberland and Westmorland*. London, 1965.

Hughes, John. *Liverpool Banks & Bankers, 1760–1837*. Liverpool, 1906.

Jensen, Arthur L. *The Maritime Commerce of Colonial Philadelphia*. Madison, Wis., 1963.

John, A. H. "Insurance Investment and the London Money Market in the 18th Century," *Economica*, n.s., 20 (1953), 137–158.

Jones, D. W. "London Overseas Merchant Groups at the End of the Seventeenth Century and the Moves against the East India Company." D.Phil. diss., Oxford University, 1970.

Jones, Theophilus. *A History of the County of Brecknock*, ed. Sir Joseph Russell Bailey and Edwin Davies. 4 vols. Brecknock, 1909–1930.

Joslin, D. M. "London Bankers in Wartime, 1739–84," in L. S. Pressnell, ed., *Studies in the Industrial Revolution Presented to T. S. Ashton*, pp. 156–177. London, 1960.

—— "London Private Bankers, 1720–1785," *Economic History Review*, 2d ser., 7 (1954), 167–186.

Land, Aubrey C. "Economic Base and Social Structure: The Northern Chesapeake in the Eighteenth Century," *Journal of Economic History*, 25 (1965), 639–654.

—— "Economic Behavior in a Planting Society: The Eighteenth Century Chesapeake," *Journal of Southern History*, 33 (1967), 469–485.

Leighton-Boyce, J. A. S. L. *Smiths the Bankers, 1658–1958*. London, 1958.

Lipson, Ephraim. *The Economic History of England,* 3d and 6th eds. 3 vols. London, 1943, 1956.

Locke, Amy A. *The Hanbury Family.* 2 vols. London, 1916.

McCusker, John J. "The Current Value of English Exports, 1697 to 1800," *William and Mary Quarterly,* 3d ser., 28 (1971), 607–628.

———— *Money and Exchange in Europe and America, 1600–1775: A Handbook.* Chapel Hill, N.C., 1978.

Mann, Julia de L. *The Cloth Industry in the West of England from 1640 to 1880.* Oxford, 1971.

Mathias, Peter. *The Brewing Industry in England, 1700–1830.* Cambridge, 1959.

———— "Capital, Credit and Enterprise in the Industrial Revolution," *Journal of European Economic History,* 2 (1973), 121–143.

Matthews, P. W., and A. W. Tuke. *History of Barclays Bank Limited.* London, 1926.

Mirowski, Philip Edward. "The Birth of the Business Cycle." Ph.D. diss., University of Michigan, 1979.

Mitchell, B. R., and Phyllis Deane. *Abstract of British Historical Statistics.* Cambridge, 1962.

Moir, E. A. L. "The Gentlemen Clothiers: A Study of the Organization of the Gloucestershire Cloth Industry, 1750–1835," in H. P. R. Finberg, ed., *Gloucestershire Studies,* pp. 225–266. Leicester, 1957.

Namier, Sir Lewis, and John Brooke. *The History of Parliament: the House of Commons 1754–1790.* 3 vols. Oxford and New York, 1964.

The New Statistical Account of Scotland. 15 vols. Edinburgh and London, 1845.

Overfield, Richard A. "The Loyalists of Maryland during the American Revolution." Ph.D. diss., University of Maryland, 1968.

Papenfuse, Edward C. *In Pursuit of Profit: The Annapolis Merchants in the Era of the American Revolution, 1763–1805.* Baltimore, Md., 1975.

Pares, Richard. "A London West-India Merchant House, 1740–1769," in R. Pares and A. J. P. Taylor, eds. *Essays Presented to Sir Lewis Namier,* pp. 75–107. London, 1956.

———— *Merchants and Planters. Economic History Review Supplement,* 4. London, 1960.

Pressnell, Leslie S. *Country Banking in the Industrial Revolution.* Oxford, 1956.

—————— "The Rate of Interest in the Eighteenth Century," in L. S. Pressnell, ed., *Studies in the Industrial Revolution Presented to T. S. Ashton*, pp. 178–214. London, 1960.

Price, F. G. Hilton. *A Handbook of London Bankers*. London, 1876; enlarged ed., 1890–1891.

Price, Jacob M. *France and the Chesapeake: A History of the French Tobacco Monopoly, 1674–1791, and of Its Relationship to the British and American Tobacco Trades*. 2 vols. Ann Arbor, Mich., 1973.

—————— "Joshua Johnson in London, 1771–1775," in Anne Whiteman, J. S. Bromley, and P. G. M. Dickson, eds., *Statesmen, Scholars and Merchants: Essays . . . Presented to Dame Lucy Sutherland*, pp. 153–180. Oxford, 1973.

—————— "A Note on the Value of Colonial Exports of Shipping," *Journal of Economic History*, 26 (1976), 704–724.

—————— "One Family's Empire: The Russell-Lee-Clerk Connection in Maryland, Britain, and India, 1707–1857," *Maryland Historical Magazine*, 72 (1977), 165–225.

—————— "The Rise of Glasgow in the Chesapeake Tobacco Trade, 1707–1775," *William and Mary Quarterly*, 3d ser., 11 (1954), 179–199.

—————— *The Tobacco Adventure to Russia*. Transactions of the American Philosophical Society, n.s., 51, pt. 1. Philadelphia, Pa., 1961.

—————— "The Tobacco Trade and the Treasury." Ph.D. diss., Harvard University, 1954.

—————— "Who Was John Norton?" *William and Mary Quarterly*, 3d ser., 19 (1962), 400–407.

Rainbolt, John C. *From Prescription to Persuasion: Manipulation of Eighteenth Century Virginia Economy*. Port Washington, N.Y., 1974.

[Reid, Robert, et al.]. *Glasgow Past and Present*, new ed. 3 vols. Glasgow, 1884.

Rosenblatt, Samuel M. "The Significance of Credit in the Tobacco Trade: A Study of John Norton & Sons, 1768–1775," *William and Mary Quarterly*, 3d ser., 19 (1962), 383–399.

Sayers, Richard S. *Lloyds Bank in the History of English Banking*. Oxford, 1957.

Shapiro, Seymour. *Capital and the Cotton Industry*. Ithaca, N.Y., 1967.

Sheridan, Richard B. "The British Credit Crisis of 1772 and the American Colonies," *Journal of Economic History*, 20 (1960), 161–186.

Simpson, Alan. *The Wealth of the Gentry, 1540–1660: East Anglian Studies.* Cambridge and Chicago, 1961.

Soltow, James H. "Scottish Traders to Virginia," *Economic History Review,* 2d ser., 12 (1959), 83–98.

Stewart, George. *Curiosities of Glasgow Citizenship.* Glasgow, 1881.

Supple, Barry E. *Commercial Crisis and Change in England, 1600–1642.* Cambridge, 1959.

———— *The Royal Exchange Assurance: A History of British Insurance, 1720–1970.* Cambridge, 1970.

Sutherland, Lucy S. "Sir George Colebrook's World Corner in Alum, 1771–3," *Economic History: A Supplement to the Economic Journal,* 3 (1936), 237–258.

———— *A London Merchant, 1695–1774.* London, 1933, 1962.

Tawney, R. H. "Introduction," in Thomas Wilson, *A Discourse upon Usury,* pp. 3–172. New York and London, 1925.

U.S. Bureau of the Census. *A Century of Population Growth . . . 1790–1900.* Washington, D.C., 1909.

———— *Historical Statistics of the United States, Colonial Times to 1957.* Washington, D.C., 1960.

———— *Historical Statistics of the United States, Colonial Times to 1970.* 2 vols. Washington, D.C., 1976.

Wells, Robert V. *The Population of the British Colonies in America before 1776.* Princeton, N. J., 1975.

Westerfield, Ray Bert. *Early History of American Auctions: A Chapter in Commercial History.* Transactions of the Connecticut Academy of Arts and Sciences, 23. New Haven, Conn., 1920.

———— *Middlemen in English Business Particularly between 1660 and 1760.* Transactions of the Connecticut Academy of Arts and Sciences, 19. New Haven, Conn., 1915.

White, Philip L. *The Beekmans of New York in Politics and Commerce, 1647–1877.* New York, 1956.

Wilson, Charles. *Anglo-Dutch Commerce and Finance.* Cambridge, 1941.

Wilson, R. G. *Gentlemen Merchants: The Merchant Community in Leeds, 1700–1830.* Manchester and New York, 1971.

Woodhead, J. R. *The Rulers of London, 1660–1689.* London, 1965.

Index